BELGO
COOKBOOK

DENIS BLAIS AND ANDRÉ PLISNIER

BELGO
COOKBOOK

DENIS BLAIS
AND ANDRÉ PLISNIER

PHOENIX
ILLUSTRATED

CONTENTS

FOREWORD

by MICHAEL JACKSON

LET US GET the wine-and-food question out of the way first. Where would you most readily find an impeccably selected list of fine French wines, and cuisine to match? In Brussels. No city has as many fine restaurants per head of population. Why is this so little known? Because the Belgians don't talk much about food: they demand the best, usually get it, and know it when they see it. Most often, they enjoy it with beer.

This is not always obvious. That flûte on the table: surely it contains pink Champagne? You saw a Champagne bottle being uncorked? Well, no: the bottle contained a winey-tasting aperitif, Framboise – a Lambic beer tinged with raspberries. The Burgundy sampler, full of a darker red liquid? That is Rodenbach, an oak-aged beer to cut the richest cassoulet. And that brandy snifter? It embraces the aromas of a rich, chocolatey digestif beer from a Trappist monastery.

A Belgian Trappist monk, who apparently has his own code of denial, once insisted that I try his beer with asparagus. In Belgium, lovers of that seasonal speciality are also inclined to dine off hop shoots prepared in much the same way. Fortunately, they leave sufficient hops to spice their beer.

Beer to arouse the appetite for a meal that will be delicate in flavours but hearty in portion. Beer as an ingredient in the dish; not just in steamed mussels or carbonade flamande, but in countless other dishes – even in desserts. Beer as an accompaniment and as a digestif. There is a sense of relish here that can be recognized in the paintings of Bruegel, where beer and food are served with a generosity to tempt the gods. The sensuous land of Rubens, the surrealistic *terroir* of Magritte, has a rich creativity.

I once spoke at a dinner in New York prepared by four Belgian chefs, boasting between them six Michelin stars. Most of the dishes were prepared with beer, and we had a different brew with each course. The Belgians call this *cuisine à la bière*. It is not the whole story of their kitchen, any more than moules and frites are (though that is surely one of the world's classically simple meals, especially with a glass of the beer called Gueuze).

For years, I have spoken and written about the joys of Belgian beer and food, but Denis and André have made this wonderful combination available in Britain. Now, they have a word of subversive advice: *Do* try this at home.

DO TRY THIS AT HOME.

Michael Jackson, presenter of television's The Beer Hunter, *is author of* The Beer Companion *and* The Great Beers of Belgium, *and winner of the Mercurius Award, presented by Crown Prince Philippe of Belgium.*

THE Belgo EXPERIENCE...

I N 1986 – when Belgium managed to make it past the World Cup quarter finals by defeating the Soviet Union – we were probably the only two guys in South Kensington waving the Belgian flag who didn't work at the Embassy. Lonesomely celebrating this historic Belgian victory, we set our minds on finding a restaurant that would serve a large casserole of *moules* with crispy *frites* and lashings of mayonnaise. We had to settle for a lukewarm pint of Stella Artois and a bag of soggy chips. That night we made a promise to bring the Moules-Frites-Bières experience to London.

We spent the next six years trying to convince banks and investors that London was in great need of a Belgian restaurant serving unpretentious traditional food. With the heydays of the Eighties long dead, a major recession, and London restaurants going bust every five minutes, we had our work cut out. Our biggest obstacle was investment. But our second one was Belgium: people simply laughed at us. Belgium's image in the UK was hardly as fashionable as Italy, Spain or California, and potential investors were very sceptical about mussels being the main feature on our menu. "The English will not eat mussels", they said. Sorry chaps – you were wrong!

It took the consumption of a few more stale Stellas before Belgo opened its doors to the Camden public in April 1992. Eighteen months later we had to double the seating capacity of the restaurant. In April 1995 we opened the 400-seat beer hall and restaurant Belgo Centraal in Covent Garden. It seems that if Belgium achieves any success in the next World Cup we will have one hell of a whoop in our two restaurants. And there will be plenty of mussels and chips and Belgian beers to go round this time!

Designing and packaging the Belgo concept was a real challenge, taking into consideration the Belgian image problem and general lack of interest. We love Belgium's food and all its quirkiness. We love the jokes and we love the beers. For us that's all we needed to be convinced that Belgo would work. And besides, the British always love an underdog.

Belgium's historical culinary and cultural background played a major role in preparing the "briefs" for the design teams of both Belgo restaurants. The original Belgo on Chalk Farm Road, a monastic refectory with wooden brewery-style tables and staff in Trappist monk-like habits, was inspired by Belgium's strong brewing tradition and the simplicity of its food. The high-tech feel was attributed to the fact that although Belgium is deeply rooted in its traditional past it now plays a very important role in the artistic and the political landscaping of a Europe in the 1990s. Anand Zenz, the designer of Belgo Noord, was highly successful in his eccentric interpretation of the European brewery eating hall, designing pick-axe-handled tables and chairs, and a mechanomorphic kitchen air extraction system. The concrete rendered walls and façade are there to remind us of the concrete sea barricades from Oostende to Blankenberge. The striking and often comical lettering embedded into the

Belgo
NOORD

Belgo
CENTRAAL

restaurant walls are medieval names for common fayre, mainly fish, from Rabelais' *Pantagruel* and *Gargantua*, such as Donkeythistle, Tumturdy and Thornback. This was a rather ingenious way to avoid having to hang obvious Bruegel and Magritte reproductions on the walls. It also gave the restaurant a certain peasantish and festive atmosphere.

Belgo Noord's later extension, designed by the world-renowned Ron Arad, experimented with external forms and interior space. The result was a reinvention of the Biergarten concept, with acid-etched steel and plywood beams soaring in and out of a glass roof, mirror-finish table tops, and a dyed-concrete base bar complete with an amoeba-shaped wooden top.

Back in Covent Garden, the 12,000 square feet of Belgo Centraal provided the sheer size that the Belgo concept has always deserved. Work on the site began in November 1994 and Ron Arad and Associates were commissioned to create a Belgo themed on Belgium's central geographical position in Europe incorporating high-volume transit and, of course, the brewing trade. The result here was of sheer industrious, machine-like, wonder.

There are two separate eating halls. One is for people on the go – no reservations are required and diners can sit on their own or with a party of ten in this 350-seat "beerhall". The second, like a modern continental train station waiting room, promotes the stop-over rather than the usual Covent Garden restaurant rush hour and has a more intimate setting. Belgo Centraal's entrance is no exception to the transit concept, linking Shelton Street to Earlham Street by a bridge that crosses over the kitchens. A lift takes diners one floor down to the traffic of food runners and rolling barrels, where chefs' shouts echo station announcements.

The six years spent preparing the Belgo "package" were not used up focusing solely on the design and architectural aspects of the projects. As a matter of fact, 70% of our time was concentrated on researching the food and drink of Belgium: the heart and soul of Belgo. André, being Belgian, was brought up with delights such as *moules et frites* and *waterzooi de poulet* and for him it was a childhood dream to be able have a restaurant that would feature all his family's favourite recipes. Denis, having lived for five years on the Continent, mainly in Cologne, was desperate to have a brewery-style restaurant, that served unpretentious and inexpensive food with superb quality beers. Belgium was calling!

Much to our delight, Belgo was an instant success. We have been asked on numerous occasions to define the key to this success and we always reply: The food that we serve is delicious and affordable, and our unique Belgian beer selection is the best in Britain.

A traditional Belgian cuisine cookery book was definitely needed in the English language. So, when the offer came to do this book, we felt we not only had the golden opportunity to assemble all the delicious recipes of Belgo's favourite dishes, but also the challenge to make a cookery book exciting. Our apologies go to all the cookery book fans out there, but we always felt that, for average Joes like us, cookery books were nice to look at but unusable or incomprehensible. We hope we've changed that with this book by creating a guide to the strange world of day-to-day Belgo-isms and easy-to-use recipes using simple accessible ingredients.

The *Belgo Cook Book* is a compilation of the best-loved dishes we have served in Belgo. It includes all the Belgian traditional favourites such as *waterzooi de poulet* and *carbonade flamande* but the main accent is on the

Moules &

+

Frites & Bière

2,000 METRIC TONS OF MUSSELS LATER...

cuisine à la bière and moules et frites, the true national dish of Belgium. Oh yes, we have even included our secret recipe for our chips.

We have tried to keep the layout of this book similar to our menus. In true Belgo fashion we made sure the design would be as you've never seen before – and yet familiar and user-friendly, making it easy to follow, especially to the Belgo fanatics that we see week after week, year in year out.

You should have no trouble finding most of the raw ingredients recommended in our recipes. Items such as celeriac (celery root) can now be found in any good supermarket. Special potatoes, like the Bintjes, mentioned on page 42, can also be ordered from good food merchants.

All the Belgian beers and genevers in this book can be purchased directly from Belgo. Cooking with beer may seem unusual to some – especially with fish – but it is a method that has been used for centuries in Flanders and Wallonia with tasty results. We tend to laugh when some of the press refer to Belgo's food as being fashionable or even trendy. Belgium fashionable in London? (No wonder poor old King Baudouin passed away. He could finally rest in peace.) The food has been fashionable in Belgium for hundreds of years– we merely wanted to celebrate it with a wider audience. Belgian fayre is for people who want to eat it, not philosophically dissect it. We hope this book helps you make a Belgian celebration, feast or simple snack an everyday joy.

So, 2,000 metric tonnes of mussels later what is the question we most often get asked?

Q. *HOW DO YOU STILL MANAGE TO EAT MUSSELS AFTER SEEING SO MANY EVERY DAY?*

A. *WITH FRITES AND MAYO!*

(BOYS
& GIRLS,
LET'S GO)

ALLEZ PEI ET MEI

Denis & André

Moules,
Muscheln, Mosselen, Cozze, Mussels!

LOOKING FOR A FEW KILOS of high quality, clean mussels is one thing: looking for 1 tonne per day is another. At Belgo we cook up to 7 tonnes of fresh mussels per week. Part of those six years doing preparatory research was spent looking into this slightly intimidating task. But with all honesty, we pessimistically anticipated selling only some 1–2 tonnes per week, which goes to show how surprised we were with Belgo's phenomenal success. After all we were warned by the so-called experts that the British did not really appreciate mussels.

THEY WERE WRONG!

CHERCHER LA MOULE

DURING OUR INTREPID RESEARCH, part of our problem was to assure year-round supplies to both restaurants. So sourcing batches of mussels that were not spawning, or reproducing, in the mid-May through to July period, turned our search into a globe-trotting event. As a result Belgo has served fresh mussels from Canada, Denmark, Holland, Ireland, Scotland, Wales and, yes, even England. For some time now we have been using mainly Scottish rope-grown mussels that are cultivated in some of the purest waters in all of Europe, namely Ulg on the west coast of the Isle of Lewis.

Fresh, clean and well-sheltered waters are absolutely crucial for producing sweet-tasting fleshy mussels. The slightest variation in the degrees of water purity and salinity could have a huge impact on the actual taste of a mussel. After many years of scouring the sea beds, Belgo believes it has found the paradise for rope-grown mussels on Loch Roag and Loch Drovinish.

"Jock" Mackenzie, founder of Hebridean Seafoods, purchased the 10,000 acres of Saliscro Estate back in 1967. After several unsuccessful attempts Jock, his son Cree, and production manager Peter Macleod got to grips with the usual engineering difficulties that arise from suspended *mytili* culture, and eventually realized the benefits of mussel farming, over the obviously more popular Scottish salmon farming. Belgo quotes Jock's views on the beneficial differences between the two aquacultures: "Mussels feed themselves and come in their own packaging." How true! Mussels are basically "filter feeders", surviving on *phytoplanktons* and tonnes of organic detritus that are found in abundance in Loch Roag and therefore cost-effectively feed themselves.

Thanks to Jock, Cree, Peter and numerous other small Scottish mussel farms, Belgo boasts using up to a quarter of all Scottish rope-grown mussels during the season.

So, which country produces the best mussel? Size and taste will vary in different waters and most producers will wave their own flag. The French like the smallish tasty Bouchot mussel, which is cultivated on long poles or stakes driven into shallow water pools or estuaries. Irish mussels, although quite small, have a superb smoky/salty taste. Check out the Bantry Bay mussel festival in mid-May on the south-west coast and while you're down there say hello to John Murphy of Fastnet Mussels. The Dutch and the Belgians will pay outrageous prices for their large "Goulden" mussels that are mainly grown on state-distributed mussel beds on the bottom of the world's most famous mussel growing pools, the Escaut, off the shores of Yerseke in Holland. Koe Prins, the mussel producer "king", claims his outfit, Prins and Dingemans, can produce up to 50,000 kilos per day. Perhaps ... but Jan of Anderssens in Agessund Denmark can dredge up to 100,000 kilos of the super-large wild Danish mussels that grow on the world's largest natural mussel farm, the Limfjord. Having said that, most of Denmark's delicious mussels are used for processing: in tins, jars, and frozen. And guess who owns most of Anderssens? You got it: The Dutch mussel "king" himself. The Scots have supplied Belgo year round because of the quality and freshness of their

MUSSELS FEED THEMSELVES AND COME IN THEIR OWN PACKAGING

produce, so hats off to Jock Mackenzie and co.

So, which country produces the most mussels? Sorry Jock and Bonny Scotland, we're afraid you're a little out of your mussel-pot depth with on this one. Spain produces some 200,000 tonnes per year. Holland follows with 100,000, Italy 80,000, France 70,000, Germany 50,000, Ireland 20,000, Greece 15,000 and the UK 7,000 tonnes per year. But enough of the mussel olympics!

So is bigger better? A good-sized mussel will have up to 28–30% mussel meat weight content and usually takes up to two years to grow. At Belgo we use different sizes for different serving styles. In our one kilo mussel pots we will use an average minimum meat weight size of 28% . Our mussel platters require a larger sized mussel of at least 30% and that's because they are first blanched or cooked just enough to open before grilling. Hence the larger meat content remains substantial when serving the dish. These large "Jumbo" mussels can take three to four years to grow and can reach up to 45% meat weight content. Belgo recommends the medium size mussel simply because the mussel texture and taste is at its best in the early parts of its second year. At that age they are known as spats or juvenile mussels.

Wild mussels can spawn from May to September and are collected or they settle on long ropes that hang down from flotation rafts. The best time to collect the spats are from mid-April to mid-July. They cling on to these long polypropylene ropes for the rest of their sweet, dear lives. These little spats need quite a lot of expert attention. Routine check-ups on them include stock density, water temperature, and removal of marine fouling such as seasquirts and seastars. The greatest threat is Red Tide, a discoloration caused by algae that raises the toxicity in the water, thus cutting off the mussels' oxygen and making the crustacean dangerously poisonous. But have no fear! Firstly, the mussels sort themselves out once the Red Tide passes by filtering themselves. Secondly, all farmed mussels are cultivated in strictly-monitored waters, usually by the State itself. Any signs of toxicity in the waters will be immediately identified and all farmers will then subsequently be forbidden to continue cultivation. All mussels should be grown in Grade A waters. If they are not they will need fresh sea-water purification treatment before they are sold on to the market.

GET RID OF THAT BEARD!

How do these large fresh mussel producers manage to de-beard, or de-biste as it's more commonly known in the trade, the tonnes of mussels that are on demand daily? Huge conveyor belt-like channels, pumped with chilled sea water, drive and rinse the just-landed "grapes" of mussels before they are re-directed onto another belt with small permeated stainless steel rollers that continuously roll in opposite directions catching the mussel beard and tearing it off. *Ouch* times 10 tonnes. The mussels are then dropped onto sorting machines which shake the freshly "shaved" mussels onto a bed of pipes with gaps in between them that vary in size. The mussels eventually find their own way into their appropriate basket-sized and awaiting bagging and tagging. Tag names vary according to size: Extras, Supers, Imperials, Jumbos, Goldens.

Q. *WHAT DO YOU CALL A BABY MUSSEL?*

A. *A BRUSSEL!*

Here are Denis and André's
MUSSEL TIPS AND MYTHS:

1 Smell the mussels you are about to purchase. Look out for any that are gasping and have an overly-strong, pungent fishy smell. A fresh bag of mussels will smell of the sea and nothing else.

2 Rope-grown mussels have thinner body meat and tend to be sweeter in taste. Because their shells tend to be thinner, you might find more crushed or dead mussels, which you should discard. Rope-grown mussels require less cleaning time and should be totally grit free.

3 Bottom cultured or dredged mussels are usually purified in large holding tanks. During that process all impurities, sand or grit should be removed. If they have clean shells it means that they have been through this process. If you are purchasing local mussels and they appear very dirty, make sure you give them a good rinse under very cold water (seawater if available). Do not let them sit in a sink full of tap water as this will eventually drown them,

4 Remove the beard of the mussel by pinching and pulling. Do not remove the beard unless you plan to cook the mussels straight away. De-bearding lowers the mussels' shelf life. Mussels may have up to five days shelf life if they are stored under the correct conditions.

5 If a mussel opens up prior to cooking tap it on a hard surface. It should close itself . If it doesn't, discard it.

6 If a mussel does not open once you've cooked it, do not eat it.

7 Like pasta, mussels can be served with thousands of different sauces. So get your chef's hat on and create.

8 Mussel Art: *Casserole and Closed Mussels,* 1964, by Marcel Broodthaers, in the Tate Gallery, London.

9 Mussels are one of the heathiest food stuffs on earth. They are packed with minerals, high in protein and very low in saturated fats. They are supposedly the best thing for the common cold.

10 Before hand-picking mussels locally, check with the water authority for water purity in that area. Hand picking is not recommended unless you are an expert.

Denis and André's
GUIDE TO COOKING MOULES

1 Cook your mussels in a large, covered pan over high heat. After 1 minute, lift the lid to release the first steam.

2 Cover again and continue cooking for 2–3 minutes more. Shake occasionally to stir the mussels.

3 After 3–4 minutes, your mussels should be all opened and ready to eat. Discard any unopened mussels.

4 Get your frites and beers ready. Start tucking away. Allez pei!!!

POTS OF MOULES

A steaming pot of mussels, accompanied by a bowl of freshly made, crisp golden frites, with creamy mayonnaise, is the heart of Belgian food. Every restaurant in Belgium has its own way of cooking mussels – some offer dozens of variations – and we, too, have our favourites.

At Belgo we serve them in a large casserole (about 3 litres / 6 pints capacity) with a deep lid to collect the empty shells. It holds 1 kg / 2¼ lb of mussels, which we reckon is just right for one person - but Belgo is famous for its gargantuan helpings. Our mussel platters, (pages 33–37) were created for those with less than gargantuan appetites.

To make the final preparation as painless as possible, you can clean the mussels (see page 21) earlier in the day.

VIVE LA MOULE!

Moules à la bière et aux lardons
(Mussels with beer and bacon)

1 kg / 2¼ lb mussels, cleaned
1 small onion, chopped
½ stick of celery, chopped
50 g / 2 oz smoked bacon, cut into large dice
125 ml / 4 fl oz beer (preferably Leffe Blonde)
bouquet garni
beurre manié (2 teaspoons softened butter mashed with
    2 teaspoons plain flour until smooth)
salt and pepper

Put the mussels in a casserole with the onion, celery and 200 ml / 7 fl oz water. Place over high heat, bring to the boil and cook until the mussels have opened, stirring frequently to ensure the mussels are evenly cooked: this takes only a few minutes.

Strain the cooking liquid through a fine sieve into a measuring jug, leaving behind any grit. Discard any mussels that have not opened. Return the opened mussels, in their shells, to the casserole.

To make the sauce, fry the bacon over a very low heat until lightly browned. Drain off any excess fat, then add the beer, bouquet garni and 125 ml / 4 fl oz of the strained mussel liquid. Bring to the boil and whisk in the beurre manié to thicken the sauce slightly. Season to taste, pour over the mussels, bring back to the boil and serve at once.

VARIATION

(Mussels with Trappist ale)

Omit the bacon and replace the blonde beer with Chimay Rouge.

Moules au vin blanc
(Mussels with white wine)

1 kg / 2¼ lb mussels, cleaned
1 small onion, chopped
1 stick of celery, chopped
125 ml / 4 fl oz dry white wine
salt and pepper
1 tablespoon chopped fresh parsley

Clean and check over the mussels very thoroughly. Put them in a casserole with the onion, celery, wine and seasoning. Place over high heat, cover with a lid, bring to the boil and cook until the mussels have opened, stirring frequently to ensure they are evenly cooked: this takes only a few minutes.

Add the parsley and serve at once.

Moules bleue
(Mussels with white wine and Roquefort cheese)

1 kg / 2¼ lb mussels, cleaned
200 ml / 7 fl oz dry white wine
50 g / 2 oz Roquefort cheese

Clean and check over the mussels very thoroughly. Put them in a casserole with the wine, place over high heat, bring to the boil and cook until the mussels have opened, stirring frequently to ensure they are evenly cooked: this takes only a few minutes.

Meanwhile, cut or crumble the cheese into very small pieces. When the mussels are cooked, add the cheese gradually, stirring until it begins to melt; serve at once.

Moules marinière
(Mussels with celery, onion and garlic)

1 kg / 2¼ lb mussels, cleaned
1 small onion, sliced
1 stick of celery, sliced
1 garlic clove, chopped
50 ml / 2 fl oz water
salt and pepper
beurre manié (2 teaspoons softened butter mashed with
    2 teaspoons plain flour until smooth) – optional
1 tablespoon chopped fresh parsley

Put the mussels in a casserole with the onion, celery, garlic and water. Place over high heat, bring to the boil and cook until the mussels have opened, stirring frequently to ensure the mussels are evenly cooked: this takes only a few minutes.

Strain the cooking liquid through a sieve into a small saucepan, leaving behind any grit, and discard any mussels that have not opened. Return the opened mussels, in their shells, to the casserole.

Bring the mussel liquid to the boil and season to taste. If using the beurre manié, whisk it in to make a smooth sauce. Add the parsley and pour over the mussels in the casserole. Heat through and serve at once.

VARIATION

(Mussels with green peppercorns)

Replace the garlic with 2 tablespoons green peppercorns. In this recipe the sauce needs to be thickened with beurre manié

Moules moutarde
(Mussels with mustard and cream sauce)

1 kg / 2¼ lb mussels, cleaned

1 small onion, chopped

½ stick of celery, chopped

100 ml / 3½ fl oz dry white wine

2 teaspoons Dijon mustard

250 ml / 8 fl oz double cream

1 egg yolk

salt and pepper

1 teaspoon chopped fresh parsley or tarragon

Put the mussels in a casserole with the onion, celery, wine and 100 ml / 3½ fl oz water. Place over high heat, bring to the boil and cook until the mussels have opened, stirring frequently to ensure the mussels are evenly cooked: this takes only a few minutes.

Strain the cooking liquid through a fine sieve into a small saucepan, leaving behind any grit, and discard any mussels that have not opened. Return the opened mussels, in their shells, to the casserole.

Mix the mustard, cream and egg yolk until smooth. Bring the mussel liquid to the boil, then remove from the heat and immediately whisk in the mustard mixture to make a smooth sauce. Season to taste.

Pour the sauce over the mussels in the casserole and heat through gently (do not let the sauce boil or it will separate). Sprinkle with chopped parsley or tarragon and serve at once.

HOW TO EAT MOULES

Retain the shell from the first mussel you eat. You should use this shell as a form of pincher to pluck the rest of your mussels. So please…

NO FORKS AND KNIVES!

BELGO'S TOP 10 TUNES
TO LISTEN TO WHILE COOKING BELGIAN FOOD

1. **ET MOI, ET MOI, ET MOI** –
   Jacques Dutronc
2. **ÇA PLANE POUR MOI** –
   Plastic Bertrand
3. **JE SUIS D'ACCORD** –
   Françoise Hardy
4. **JACKY** –
   Jacques Brel
5. **69 ANNÉE EROTIQUE** –
   Serge Gainsbourg
6. **NATIONAL 7** –
   Honeymoon Killers
7. **CHERRY BLOSSOM** –
   Pepe Ramillo and the Mexican Fiesta
8. **MUSCLE OF LOVE** –
   Alice Cooper
9. **LÀ OU Y A DES FRITES** –
   Georgette Plana
10. **DOMINIQUE** –
    The Singing Nun

Moules poulette
(Mussels with mushroom, lemon and cream sauce)

1 kg / 2¼ lb mussels, cleaned
100 ml / 3½ fl oz dry white wine
25 g / 1 oz butter
125 g / 4 oz mushrooms (preferably oyster mushrooms),
  thinly sliced
250 ml / 8 fl oz double cream
juice of ½ lemon
¼ teaspoon crushed black peppercorns
salt

Clean and check over the mussels very thoroughly. Put them in a casserole with the wine and 100 ml / 3½ fl oz water, place over high heat, bring to the boil and cook until the mussels have opened, stirring frequently to ensure they are evenly cooked: this takes only a few minutes.

To make the sauce, melt the butter in a saucepan, add the mushrooms and sauté until just tender. Add the mushrooms to the mussels and bring to the boil, then stir in the cream, lemon juice, peppercorns and salt to taste. Heat through and serve at once.

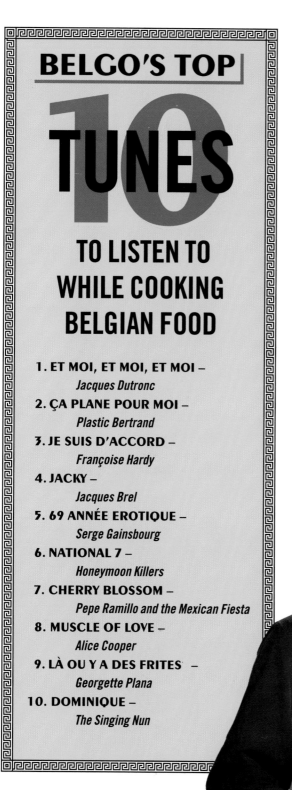

28

Moules navigateur
(Mussels with curry cream sauce)

1 kg / 2¼ lb mussels, cleaned
400 ml / 14 fl oz dry white wine
25 g / 1 oz butter
1 small onion, chopped
1 small carrot, chopped
25 g / 1 oz sultanas
½ teaspoon curry powder
½ teaspoon tomato purée
1 small apple (preferably Golden Delicious)
150 ml / 5 fl oz double cream

Put the mussels in a casserole with the wine, place over high heat, bring to the boil and cook until the mussels have opened, stirring frequently to ensure they are evenly cooked: this takes only a few minutes.

Strain the cooking liquid through a fine sieve into a jug, leaving behind any grit, and discard any mussels that have not opened. Return the opened mussels, in their shells, to the casserole; cover and set aside.

Melt the butter in a saucepan, add the onion and carrot and cook over a low heat for 2 minutes or until softened but not browned. Add the sultanas, curry powder and tomato purée and cook, stirring, for 1 minute. Gradually stir in the strained mussel liquid. Peel the apple, cut into wedges and add to the sauce. Let the sauce simmer gently for 5 minutes, then add the cream.

Pour over the mussels and heat through gently; serve at once.

Moules congo
(Mussels with coconut cream and lemongrass)

1 kg / 2¼ lb mussels, cleaned
125 ml / 4 fl oz dry white wine
50 g / 2 oz butter
1 lemongrass stalk, very finely chopped
2–3 small green chillies, finely chopped
2.5 cm / 1 inch piece of fresh ginger, peeled and finely chopped
1 small onion, very thinly sliced
1 small carrot, very thinly sliced
salt
4 tablespoons coconut cream
4 tablespoons double cream
1 teaspoon chopped fresh parsley

Put the mussels in a casserole with the wine and 150 ml / ¼ pint water, place over high heat, bring to the boil and cook for a few minutes only, until the mussels have opened, stirring frequently to ensure they are evenly cooked.

Strain the cooking liquid through a fine sieve into a jug, leaving behind any grit, and discard any mussels that have not opened. Return the opened mussels, in their shells, to the casserole; cover and set aside.

Heat the butter in a saucepan, add the lemongrass, chillies and ginger and cook over a low heat for 5 minutes. Add the onion and carrot and cook for a further 5 minutes, until softened but not browned. Add the strained mussel liquid and simmer gently for 30 minutes.

Add a pinch of salt, the coconut cream and double cream and simmer for a further 10 minutes.

Add the mussels and heat through for 2 minutes, then sprinkle with parsley and serve at once.

Moules provençale
(Mussels with tomatoes, herbs and garlic)

1 kg / 2¼ lb mussels, cleaned
100 ml / 3½ fl oz dry white wine

PROVENÇALE SAUCE
1 tablespoon olive oil
2 onions, chopped
1 stick of celery, chopped
1 garlic clove, chopped
1 teaspoon chopped fresh basil, plus extra to garnish
bouquet garni
1 tablespoon tomato purée
450 g / 1 lb ripe plum tomatoes, peeled and chopped,
    or 400 g / 14 oz canned chopped tomatoes
salt and pepper
1 teaspoon caster sugar

To make the sauce, heat the olive oil in a large saucepan, add the onions, celery, garlic, basil and bouquet garni and cook over a low heat for 5 minutes or until softened but not browned.

Mix in the tomato purée and tomatoes, salt, pepper and sugar and simmer gently for 30 minutes.

Put the mussels in a casserole with the wine and 100 ml / 3½ fl oz water. Place over high heat, bring to the boil and cook for a few minutes only, until the mussels have opened, stirring frequently to ensure they are evenly cooked.

Pour off the cooking liquid, discard any mussels that have not opened and return the opened mussels, in their shells, to the casserole.

Pour the hot tomato sauce over the mussels and heat through. Sprinkle with chopped basil and serve at once.

Moules garcia
(Mussels with shrooms and tomatoes)

provençale sauce (see left)
50 g / 2 oz butter
125 g / 4 oz wild mushrooms, thinly sliced
½ teaspoon paprika
pinch of cayenne pepper
1 kg / 2¼ lb mussels, cleaned
100 ml / 3½ fl oz dry white wine
1 teaspoon chopped fresh parsley

First make the provençale sauce and set aside. Melt the butter in a saucepan, add the mushrooms and sauté for 3–4 minutes or until just tender. Add the paprika and cayenne pepper, then add the provençale sauce and heat through.

Meanwhile, put the mussels in a casserole with the wine and 100 ml / 3½ fl oz water. Place over high heat, bring to the boil and cook for a few minutes only, until the mussels have opened, stirring frequently to ensure they are evenly cooked.

Pour off the cooking liquid, discard any mussels that have not opened and return the opened mussels, in their shells, to the casserole.

Pour the hot sauce over the mussels and heat through. Sprinkle with parsley and serve at once.

Moules snob
(Mussels with lobster sauce)

lobster bisque (see right)
1 kg / 2¼ lb mussels, cleaned
100 ml / 3½ fl oz dry white wine

First make the lobster bisque and keep hot.

Put the mussels in a casserole with the wine and 100 ml / 3½ fl oz water. Place over high heat, bring to the boil and cook for a few minutes only, until the mussels have opened, stirring frequently to ensure they are evenly cooked.

Pour off the cooking liquid, discard any mussels that have not opened and return the opened mussels, in their shells, to the casserole.

Pour the hot lobster bisque over the mussels and serve at once.

Bisque de homard
(Lobster bisque with brandy)

shells of 2 lobsters
1 onion, roughly chopped
1 carrot, roughly chopped
25 g / 1 oz butter
25 g / 1 oz flour
1 tablespoon tomato purée
250 ml / 8 fl oz dry white wine
2 tablespoons brandy
bouquet garni
250 ml / 8 fl oz double cream
salt and pepper

Preheat the oven to 200° C / 400° F / Gas Mark 6.

Using a heavy cleaver, roughly chop the lobster shells and place in a roasting tin. Roast in the hot oven for 20 minutes, then add the onion and carrot and roast for a further 20 minutes.

Melt the butter in a large saucepan, add the roasted lobster shells, onion and carrot, and the flour and tomato purée. Stir well to blend evenly.

Meanwhile, deglaze the roasting tin by adding the white wine and brandy and stirring to loosen the residue in the tin. Tip this liquid into the saucepan, together with 2 litres / 3½ pints water and the bouquet garni. Bring to the boil, then simmer gently for 1½ hours until reduced by about two-thirds.

Strain into a clean saucepan, taste and simmer for a little longer if necessary to concentrate the flavour. Stir in the cream and season to taste.

31

MOULES PLATTERS

Basic preparation of platters

500 g / 1 lb 2 oz large mussels, cleaned
100 ml / 3½ fl oz dry white wine

Put the mussels in a casserole with the wine and 100 ml / 3½ fl oz water. Place over high heat, bring to the boil and cook for a few minutes only, until the mussels have opened, stirring frequently to ensure they are evenly cooked.

Strain the cooking liquid through a fine sieve into a jug, leaving behind any grit.

Put the mussels in a large bowl with plenty of ice cubes and cover with cold water to cool them as quickly as possible. Rejecting any mussels that have not opened, or that have broken shells, open each mussel, discarding the empty half shell.

Arrange the mussels on the platter, cover with clingfilm and keep in the refrigerator, well away from uncooked meat, poultry and fish.

Moules escargot (Garlic and herb butter)

1 mussel platter (see left)
100 g / 3½ oz butter
2 garlic cloves, crushed
1 tablespoon chopped fresh parsley
splash of Pernod
salt and pepper
wedge of lemon, to serve

Cut the butter into small pieces, place in a bowl and leave at room temperature for 30 minutes.

Add the garlic, parsley, Pernod and seasoning and mix together, using a fork.

Take the mussel platter from the refrigerator and dot with the flavoured butter, then place under a hot grill for 3 minutes. Serve at once, with a lemon wedge.

Moules ardennaise
(Ham, chicory and cheese)

1 mussel platter (see page 33)
1 large or 2 small heads of chicory
50 g / 2 oz butter
40 g / 1½ oz caster sugar
salt and pepper
freshly grated nutmeg
50 ml / 2 fl oz dry white wine
75 ml / 3 fl oz double cream
50 g / 2 oz Ardennes ham, cut into very thin strips
50 g / 2 oz cheese, grated

Cut the chicory in half lengthways, cut out the core and then slice thinly. Melt the butter in a wide saucepan, add the chicory, sugar, salt, pepper and nutmeg and cook over a low heat for 10 minutes.

Add the wine to the chicory and continue cooking until the liquid has reduced by half, then add the cream and ham and cook for a further 2 minutes.

Take the mussel platter from the refrigerator and spoon the sauce over the mussels. Sprinkle with the cheese, then place under a hot grill for 3–4 minutes or until golden. Serve at once.

Moules pastis
(Fennel, cream and Pernod)

1 mussel platter (see page 33)
50 g / 2 oz butter
½ fennel bulb, trimmed and finely chopped
½ onion, finely chopped
2 tablespoons Pernod
75 ml / 3 fl oz double cream
salt and pepper
50 g / 2 oz cheese, grated

Melt the butter in a saucepan, add the fennel and onion and cook over a low heat, stirring frequently, for 10 minutes, until the fennel and onion are softened but not browned.

Stir in the Pernod, cream and seasoning and cook for a further 10 minutes.

Take the mussel platter from the refrigerator and spoon the sauce over the mussels. Sprinkle with the cheese, then place under a hot grill for 3–4 minutes or until golden. Serve at once.

Moules pizza
(Tomatoes, herbs and cheese)

1 mussel platter (see page 33)
250 ml / 8 fl oz provençale sauce (see page 30)
50 g / 2 oz cheese, grated
sprigs of basil, roughly torn

Take the mussel platter from the refrigerator and spoon the sauce over the mussels. Sprinkle with the cheese, then place under a hot grill for 3–4 minutes or until golden brown. Sprinkle the basil over the platter and serve at once.

Moules poulette
(Mushrooms, lemon and cream)

1 mussel platter (see page 33)
20 g / ¾ oz butter
75 g / 3 oz mushrooms (preferably oyster mushrooms),
    thinly sliced
beurre manié (1 teaspoon softened butter mashed with
    1 teaspoon plain flour until smooth)
175 ml / 6 fl oz double cream
juice of ¼ lemon
¼ teaspoon crushed black peppercorns
salt
50 g / 2 oz cheese, grated

Prepare the mussel platter, reserving the cooking liquid.

Melt the butter in a saucepan, add the mushrooms and sauté until just tender. Bring the mussel liquid to the boil and whisk in the beurre manié. Stir in the cream, lemon juice, peppercorns and salt to taste.

Take the mussel platter from the refrigerator and spoon the sauce over the mussels until they are generously covered. Sprinkle with the cheese, then place under a hot grill for 3–4 minutes or until golden brown. Serve at once.

Moules espagnole
(Olive oil and garlic)

1 mussel platter (see page 33)
2 garlic cloves
125 ml / 4 fl oz olive oil
1 large sprig of thyme
salt and pepper
wedge of lemon, to serve

Peel the garlic and crush it under the blade of a large knife, then place it in a small bowl. Mix in the olive oil, thyme leaves and seasoning.

Take the mussel platter from the refrigerator and spoon the oil mixture generously over the mussels, making sure they are all covered. Place under a hot grill for 2 minutes. Serve at once, with a lemon wedge.

Moules meunière
(Pan-fried with lemon and butter)

1 mussel platter (see page 33)
1 lemon
50 g / 2 oz plain flour
25 g / 1 oz butter
salt and pepper
1 teaspoon chopped fresh parsley

Take the platter from the refrigerator and remove the mussels from their shells, leaving the shells on the platter.

Cut a wedge of lemon to garnish, then squeeze the juice from the remaining lemon and set aside.

Toss the mussels in the flour to coat them evenly, then shake off any excess.

Melt the butter in a frying pan until light brown. Add the mussels and fry for 2–3 minutes, until the mussels are golden brown. Return the mussels to their shells on the platter.

Add the lemon juice, seasoning and parsley to the butter in the pan, stir to deglaze, then pour the lemon butter over the mussels and serve at once, with the lemon wedge.

Moules po'pei
(Spinach and bacon)

1 mussel platter (see page 33)
125 g / 4 oz fresh spinach
salt and pepper
25 g / 1 oz butter
1 small shallot, chopped
1 garlic clove, chopped
75 ml / 3 fl oz double cream
freshly grated nutmeg
50 g / 2 oz cheese, grated

Wash the spinach thoroughly. Bring a large
saucepan of water to the boil, add a pinch of salt
and the spinach and boil for 2 minutes. Drain
and run cold water over the spinach for 2
minutes, until it is cold. Squeeze the spinach
well to remove as much water as possible.

Melt the butter in a saucepan, add the
shallot and garlic and cook over a low heat for
2 minutes. Add the cream, salt, pepper and
nutmeg and simmer gently for 10 minutes.

Meanwhile, chop the spinach very finely. Add
the spinach to the sauce and cook for 2 minutes.

Take the mussel platter from the refrigerator
and spoon the sauce over the mussels. Sprinkle with
the cheese, then place under a hot grill for 3–4
minutes or until golden. Serve at once.

FRITES, FRIETEN, FRITAS, Chips!

THE FRENCH, THE ENGLISH and the Spanish all claim not only to have invented the chip or frite, but also to have the best tasting ones. If the future of the European Union were to be decided on the outcome of this most serious debate, the Euro MPs would surely play it safe and do as always: award the honour to Belgium. But this time not for the usual practicality of avoiding huge jingoistic ego battles by giving the "little neutral country" the medal, but simply because anybody who has ever spent any time in Brussels, or Belgium for that matter, would never second guess this decision.

IS THERE LIFE ON MARS? YOU BET!

BOUFFEUR DES FRITES: THE GREAT DEBATE

WHEN IT COMES TO discussing the *Best Frites in the World Award*, there is more than one country that would like to claim not only the title but also the recognition for creating this great gastronomic delight. The French, the Spanish and, naturally, the Belgians seem always only too ready to have a heated debate over the subject. The English and Irish would surely want a say, too. But when it comes to being part of the total folklore, ridiculed to the point of being recognized as *"un pays de bouffeur de frites"* (a nation of chip-eaters), Belgium must take first place at the chip counter! Indeed, it has even been said that expectant Belgian mothers develop square nipples so that their young may familiarize themselves with eating frites from an early age. Folklore does not get any worse than that.

The Belgians flatly refuse even to debate the issue, having what they feel is the historical proof and technical know-how on producing a nice crisp tasty chip and not just your average, no offence intended, "oil sponge".

Now, if Hercule Poirot were to investigate he would immediately attract protests for the simple fact that he is Belgian. Well sort of…we are talking about a fictitious character here. OK then, so let's use André Plisnier, Belgo's own Private Investigator. He's the son of a Belgian father and an English mother who spends most her time in Spain and who has a French step-sister in Paris.

LOOKING BACK… A BRIEF HISTORY

Extreme climates, civil and religious warfare, all had a devastating impact on the basically prosperous Low Countries economy. But more importantly, these had some drastic effects on the agricultural front, thus changing people's eating and drinking habits. It was time to make some sacrifices. In short, poor wheat crops made bread hard to produce and the "easy to grow" potato became a wonder veg. Wine became unaffordable so beer (made from barley) stepped in.

The frying of foods is a technique that is believed to have originated from the Mediterranean countries. Hence it could be that the Spaniards introduced the "frying factor" to the besieged Belgians. But the real spud experts were the Lowlanders. The first ever recorded recipes using potatoes date back to 1604. They were written by a Belgian named Lancelot de Casteau.

WHERE DID YOU GET THAT *PAPAS RADIX?*

The vegetable in question is of South American origin. Its route to Europe belongs to many different tales from as many countries. As far back as the end of the 16th century the potato was grown within the confines of monasteries in Spain and Italy. But it was not being taken seriously as a food substance. Indeed it was only when the monks from these monasteries discovered medicinal benefits in the use of this vegetable that botanists, such as Jules Charles de L'Ecluse, started to pay attention.

Mr. de L'Ecluse (a.k.a. Carolus Clusius) was born in France but studied in Louvain, Ghent and finally Antwerp, where in 1601 he published his findings on the possibilities the *pomme de terre* offered and its nutritional values.

Carolus used the fertile conditions of Flemish soils to

OR

proceed with potato experimentation. There was, needless to say, a great need for an organic food supplement in Northern Europe.

THE DEVELOPMENT OF THE *FRITE*

An historian by the name of Jo Gerard found a manuscript in his family archives that dated back to 1781. It was somewhat strangely entitled *"Curiosités de la table dans les Pays-Bas Belges"* which roughly translated means "Curious dishes from the Belgian Low Countries". We quote:

"The inhabitants of Namur, Ardennes, and Dinant have the habit of frying small fish, which they catch in the Meuse, to improve their diet, specially the poor and needy. But when the frost comes and immobilizes the flow of the river, making fishing far to dangerous, the natives cut wedges of potatoes in the shape of little fish and fry them just like they would do with the fish. If I remember well this practice dates back over at least one hundred years…"

This appears to be the first recorded document that mentions the frying of potatoes. It could well be that the Spaniards took the idea of *patatas fritas* back home with them when Spanish rule ended in Belgium in the early 18th century. Having been rulers over the Belgians, they may have decided no one would argue their claim of invention or that no one would be as interested as, in fact, we are.

Great Britain imported potatoes from the Low Countries in the mid-18th century and at that time had barely started home production. The frying of foods did not catch on in Great Britain as fast as it did on the Continent. So the British claim to the first chip would seem somewhat weak.

As far as the French are concerned, Antoine Parmentier introduced the *pomme de terre* to France in 1780. They didn't start intensive cultivation there until the mid-19th century, therefore substantially weakening *their* claim.

SO, WHO MADE THE DISCOVERY?

Results for historical claim of invention:

BRITAIN:	**0**
FRANCE:	**0**
SPAIN:	**1**
BELGIUM(LC):	**1**

…AND THE NETHER NETHERLANDS…

So far the Dutch have been kept out of this *frite* investigation primarily because the potato was being cultivated mainly where Belgium is situated today. Also thousands of rich, well-to-do Flemings with all the *frite* know-how took most of their money and know-how to Amsterdam when fleeing the Spanish Inquisition and Philip II's reign of terror.

The following joke rather nicely sums up the Belgo-Dutch relationship using the *frite* as common ground:

"If you see a dead man clutching a *cornet de frites* (packet of chips) you know he's a Belgian. If you see a man nicking that packet of chips off the dead man then you know he's a Dutchman."

THE TASTE CHALLENGE

The Belgian Frite

The Belgians go a long way to ensure their *frites* are of top quality. They start by using the Bintjes potato renowned for its tartness and richness. It does not turn too floury on frying and holds its firmness perfectly. The size of the Belgian *frite* is also very important. It is said that the perfect Belgian chip should be cut to 1 cm on each side (*sur chaque coté*) and be 6 cm long.

The next part of the secret is the most important and is definitely a Belgian invention. In the mid-19th century a certain Mr. Coudelier from Ghent recorded his technique of *"double friture"*, or two-step frying procedure. The first part of frying the freshly cut chip (which has been soaked in unsalted water first) is to blanche or cook just the inside of the potato. The correct size of *frite* should blanche easily at 140°C (275°F) to 150°C (300°F) in vegetable oil. One must let the *frites* cool off completely before the second stage of frying which should be at the much higher heat of 180°C (350°F) to 185°C (360°F) until the *frites* are golden.

Belgian housewives' secrets for perfect *frite* cooking range from using only beef-dripping (which was used when oil was unaffordable) to dropping a small piece of nutmeg or a fresh vanilla pod into the oil to enhance flavour and aroma. Belgian *frites* are mostly served with mayonnaise but were originally served with pickle (something similar to piccalilli) before the French influence.

The Spanish Patatas Fritas

This is usually a larger cut *frite*, or even a wedge of potato, and depending on the oil that will be used it can have a wonderful flavour, although *fritas* tend to be a bit on the floury side.

The British Chip

The SBC (Standard British Chip) usually gets too much salt, and attention to the type of potato is often neglected. The result is often a chip that will rapidly go soggy, oily and floury. Serving the chip with a dousing of a good malt vinegar helps though.

The French Frite

The French *frite,* cut very thin, is very pleasant and is at first also quite firm and crispy. But it will, due to its thinness, go limp quite quickly. These are also served with mayonnaise if you ask for it. By the way, mayonnaise is a French invention thought to have been conceived at a celebration of the capture of Port Mahon, capital of Minorca, by the French in 1756. It was originally called Mahonnaise. (There are similar stories of Bayonnaise and Mayennaise: the first after a victory in Bayonne, where ham comes from, the other after the Duke of Mayenne, who also claims to be the inventor. Let the French argue over this one.)

Never ask a Belgian the time when he/she is eating their cornet de frites

42

"French Fries"?

Many Americans and Canadians fought in Belgium during the great battles of the Second World War. They were totally unfamiliar with the fried potato wedge. As poor old Belgium was struggling to make ends meet through this rather turbulent period in history, the *frites* kept the nation and its saviours/conquerors fed. The *fritkot* or chip wagons everywhere were the most popular restaurants in Belgium and became instant temporary landmarks. And it seems that most were manned by Belgian soldiers, who had to officially speak French according to the rules of what was left of the Belgian Army. So these fresh-faced, not-so-hot on geography Yanks and Canucks were hearing these French-speaking chaps frying up these potato slices and one thing must have led to the other. Hence "French fries". So the legend goes. It's a shame to spoil the story, but the term "French fries" was in fact already used in the 19th century.

THE RESULT OF
THE CHIPS-FRITES-FRITAS-
FRIETEN TASTE CHALLENGE:
(Points scale 0 to 5, 5 for PERFECT!)

Belgium:	4
Spain:	1
Britain:	2
France:	3

Inspector Belgo notes that Belgium wins.

Note that Belgium does not get a perfect score. (So there is such a thing as justice in the chip Olympics. Watch that judge from Norway with that 4.9 score…) The reason being that, as in most large cities, demand and profit margins put too much pressure on tradition. Hence most of Brussels' *fritures* or *fritkots* will unfortunately use frozen frites. *Fritkots* are ubiquitous so if you want true Belgian frites you should be careful. It has been said that "there are more chip wagons in Brussels than phone booths!"

So that you don't get a false impression, Belgo will give you a real insider's guide to the best *fritures* and *fritkots* of Brussels.

BELGO'S TOP 3 BRUSSELS *FRITURES* & *FRITKOTS*

1. La Fritkot à Martin:
This is in front of the beautiful Église de St. Josse on the corner of rues St. Josse and Verbist. Martin inherited this totally unpretentious chip wagon from his parents and is usually open till 7pm weekdays and later at weekends.

2. La Friture St. Antoine:
Established in 1948 it is located at Place Jourdan in Etterbeeck. The taxi drivers' favourite, this used to be a *kot* but with success came expansion.

3. La friture de la gare de Uccle:
For your last-minute late night snack and a bit of action check out this old Brussels train stop. Good *frikadellen* (meatballs) too.

Denis and André's
GUIDE TO COOKING FRITES

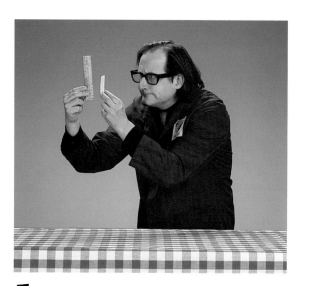

1 The perfect Belgian frite should be 1 cm on each side and 6 cm long.

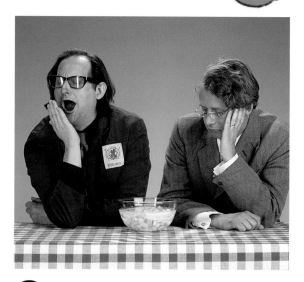

2 Soak freshly cut frites in cold water for 10–15 minutes to wash off starch.

150° C

3 The most important step is the "double friture", which means frying twice: first at 150°C.

180° C

4 Let the frites cool completely before frying for the second time at 180°C.

5 Once your frites are crispy and golden brown, salt lightly and dip in Belgian mayonnaise to have a real treat. Allez!

Bière,
Bier, Birra, Cerveza, Beer!

IF THE FRENCH BELIEVE that life is merely "something that happens between meals", it could be said that Belgians believe that "beers are the essence of life itself". One of our aims at Belgo was to introduce a beer-drinking culture that would enlighten the British public on the wide variety of Belgian beers available and develop interest in their versatility in combination with great food. We felt that good restaurant menus were not promoting beers and that wines were generally getting far too much credit. With over 650 Belgian beers to choose from, we knew Belgo would be able to create a beer menu that would tempt even the most confirmed beer-o-phobe.

WELCOME TO BEER PARADISE!

A BRIEF HISTORY OF BELGIAN BEERS

WERE THE PYRAMIDS BUILT WITH BEER?

It is believed that beer was first fermented by Egyptian slaves using bread and water. We would not go as far to state that "beer built the Pyramids", but we sure would like to!

CHEERS CAESAR!

Beer has been brewed in Belgium ever since the days of the Roman conquest. Gauls and Romans alike enjoyed drinking a Belgian brew that was a somewhat upgraded version of the Egyptian predecessor. It was called *cervoise*.

MONKS: THE FIRST BELGIAN BREWERS

The technical knowledge needed to produce the cereals for brewing beer was concentrated within the walls of the monasteries. The 11th-century monks in the Low Countries, whose orders originated in France, had a great deal of wine-making knowledge and were somewhat astute in the sciences of those times. The monks applied some of their wine-making techniques to brewing and produced the first wholesome Belgian beers. The Affligem Monastery, for example, was brewing as far back as 1083. The Floreffe Monastery started brewing in 1121. Beer was believed to be a healthy alternative to the poor state of the drinking water. It also made fasting a whole lot more fun.

To this day, some monasteries are still brewing beer. There are six Trappist monasteries that have monks brewing beer. Five of those six are in Belgium.

BEER GUILD

The flourishing interest in brewing quickly manifested itself. A small group of Master Independent Brewers created a Guild to ensure that quality standards were adhered to. In 1450 the first Brewers' Guild of the Low Countries was established. In 1660 almost 100 Brew Masters were officially recognized by the Guild. At that point, Belgium became the most influential brewing area in Northern Europe. Apparently, more than 25% of all cereals produced in this region in the 16th century were used for beer making.

DISASTROUS FRENCH RULE

In 1796 Napoleon decreed that all monasteries should be banned and destroyed. This, needless to say, put a total end to monastery brewing. The next 40 years had a devastating affect on beer making in Belgium due to large scale civil unrest and wars. Most of the monasteries were destroyed and never rebuilt. Luckily the Chimay and Rochefort monasteries were rebuilt in the mid-19th century. Today they produce some of the world's highest-quality beers.

THE COMEBACK YEARS: THE BEER REVOLUTION

After the Brabançonne Revolt and Belgium's independence from foreign rule, the brewing industry started its own revolution. The arrival of the industrial age

and modern technology played a huge role in both bigger and better production techniques. The 19th century is recognized in Belgium as the brewery boom period or the Beer Revolution. Fortunately, spurred on by laws forbidding consumption of strong spirits, beer drinking and brewing in Belgium has further developed this cultural heritage and an ever-growing demand for beer to be exported worldwide.

THE CHERISHED CHERRY BEER

Without any strict brewing regulations like the German purity laws for beer making *(Reinheitsgebot)*, the Belgians felt free to experiment with the best natural products available. The cherries of Schaarbeek, on the outskirts of Brussels were used to assist fermentation for a rather unusual sour beer, called *gueuze* or *lambic*. At the end of the 19th century, this beer was very popular and often drunk on long summer Sunday afternoons (and indeed any other afternoon). It was known as beer champagne. Not to leave out the ladies — who were not so keen on the sour base beer — the brewers added the famous local cherries to produce the first fruit beer, *Kriek* (Flemish for cherry), which rapidly became a Brussels speciality. Later, raspberries and blackcurrants were introduced to produce some rather exciting beer tastes.

THE VAN DE VELDE REGULATION

By 1919, widespread alcoholism within work forces prompted the Belgian minister Emile Van de Velde to prohibit all sales of spirits in public bars in Belgium. This created a huge vacuum for the production of a strong alcoholic drink that was not classed as a spirit. Brewers gladly felt obliged to start producing beers strong in alcohol content. Because this law remained in affect until 1983, Belgian brewers have continued to brew very strong beers. If you look at the Belgo beer list you will find that the average beer strength is around 6.8% alcohol volume. Bush beer is at a serious 12% alcohol volume. Thank you very much Monsieur Van de Velde for putting our own work force in peril!

DON'T MENTION THE WAR!

The war years saw the invasion of foreign beers into Belgium. During the First World War, the Germans brought their Pils with them. Instead of being resentful, the Belgians were only too glad to acquire a new type of beer for their rapidly growing beer portfolio. The first Belgian Pils was brewed in 1928 by the Alken Brewery. *Danke schön!* In the Second World War, the British introduced Pale Ales and Scotch-type beers. This time Belgian brewers experimented and produced a lethally strong golden ale appropriately named Duvel, meaning 'the devil'! These new styles of brewing were particularly popular throughout the 50s and 60s.

THE 70s REVOLT AND REVIVAL

With plenty of civil unrest, strikes and huge language disputes between the Flemish and Walloons, the Belgian brewers were not about to watch from the sidelines and miss such a great marketing opportunity. The time was ripe for the revival of traditional, regional and national (flag-waving) brewing techniques. Strong "academic-style" traditional brewing fronts waged battle against mass production of the foreign-style beer. Hey, it was crazy beer names for crazy times: Kwak, Delirium Tremens, Lucifer, Barbar are just a small sample of those far-out beer brands. In 1977, Michael Jackson (the English Beer Hunter himself), was the first person to publish, in the English language, a tribute to the outstanding quality and diversity of Belgian beer making.

THE 1980s: A DECADE OF THE BELGIAN BEER.

The traditional brewing revival of the Seventies never lost it's momentum and continued to inspire the reintroduction of traditional beer craftsmanship. In 1986 the Confederation of Belgian Brewers declared the year *"L'Année de la Bière"* — the year of the beer. Catchy, eh? This created a massive press interest in brewing technology and presentation and the Belgian brewers used the platform as a springboard to launch themselves for global recognition. Exports sky-rocketed.

THE 1990s: BELGIAN BEER *ÜBER ALLES*!

Today Belgian beers are the inspiration of all new budding young brewing masters and aficionados: they are the global bench-mark for quality brewing. The recent popularity of "micro-brewers", particularly in America, was mainly inspired by the simple old and natural ways of brewing beer that have been practised in Belgium for hundreds of years. Thousands of tourists, from Japan to South Africa, visit the beer museums, monasteries and breweries of Belgium every year. We hope that Belgo shares a little responsibility in having introduced these wonderful beers to a very appreciative British public.

BELGO BEER TYPE AND PAIRIN

TYPE	BRAND	COLOUR
1. Pils	Jupiler, Maes	pale
2. White Beer	Hoegaarden	white/cloudy
3. Gueuze/Lambic	Girardin, Mort Subite	champagne gold
4. Fruit Beers	Liefmans, Belle-Vue	fruit colour
5. Pale Ales	DeKonick	copper
6. Golden Ales	Duvel	golden
7. Flemish Brown Ales	Gouden Carolus	dark brown
8. Wine Beers	Rodenbach	dark red
9. Saison	Saison Dupont	cloudy
10. Trappiste	Orval, Chimay	copper, dark
11. Abbey Style	Leffe	gold or dark
12. Specialty	Kwak	amber/orange

HART

COOKING USES	FOOD PAIRING
mussel sauce, batter	shellfish
fish sauce	seafood
stews /sauce	soft cheese
game marinade	game
stew eels	filet americain
fish sauce	freshwater fish
dessert	rabbit/chocolate
game/fowl	brown shrimp
pork/choucroute	stoemp
stews/sauces	wild mushrooms
fish sauce	seafood
sauce for fowl	game/fowl

Denis and André's
GUIDE TO POURING BEER

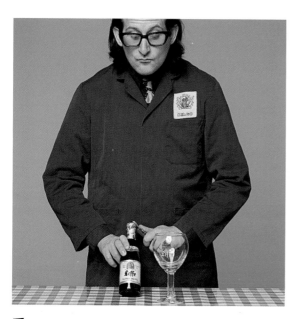

1 Open the bottle very gently so as not to disturb any sediment and allow it to breathe.

2 Inspect the glass to be sure it is clean by holding it up to the light

3 Be sure to remove any smears from around the rim and polish carefully with a clean cloth

4 Pour the nectar gently into the beautiful clean glass to ensure a good head is formed.

NOW LEVITATE JUST LIKE A MONK!

5 Drink the beer slowly, letting it sit on the palate before swallowing.

LAMBIC AND GUEUZE

LAMBIC is a very old-fashioned style of beer, made by an ancient technique that survives only in Belgium, indeed only in the area around Brussels. No yeast is added to the beer at any stage, other than the wild yeasts that fall from the air on to the cooling wort (the liquid resulting from boiling the grains, hops and water). This technique is known as spontaneous fermentation. While many of the world's beers are made entirely from malted grain (most commonly barley), lambic must contain at least 30% unmalted wheat. The hops used are not fresh hops, indeed they may be several years old: they are not added for their aroma or bitterness, as in other styles of beer, but solely for their preservative qualities.

Lambic continues to ferment and mature in wooden barrels, and emerges very still, and very sour. It is so unlike most other beers that it is considered not to be to the modern taste, and is quite rare.

Gueuze is made by blending old lambic with young lambic and then bottling it. The sugars remaining in the young lambic spark a refermentation in the bottle — very like the secondary fermentation in a bottle of Champagne. The resulting beer is sometimes called Champagne beer: it is very spritzy and is usually bottled with a Champagne cork and wire.

Gueuze is naturally sour with a hint of bitterness, and this is the way it is still made by the traditional, small, family-owned breweries. Drinkers in Belgium often add a dash of grenadine syrup to take the edge off the sourness. When bigger companies started to sell gueuze they sweetened it to make it more widely acceptable.

Whichever way you prefer it, gueuze is always refreshing and, compared to wine and other Belgian beers, low in alcohol. The Champagne-style bottle suggests that it is a good aperitif. It goes very well with lamb, chicken and apple dishes, and is an amazing partner to anything involving vinaigrette — especially the thick, herb and shallot, Belgo version.

BELLE-VUE
5.2% A comparatively sweet, widely available gueuze.

CANTILLON
5.5% A very tart, traditional gueuze.

DE TROCH
5.5% Dark in colour, this is a good example of a full-flavoured, sour gueuze. Unfortunately it is not always available from the brewery.

GIRARDIN
5% Traditional gueuze, slightly sour and citric, with lemon fruitiness and a dry, bitter finish.

MORT SUBITE
4% Light-bodied and refreshing, sweet/sour.

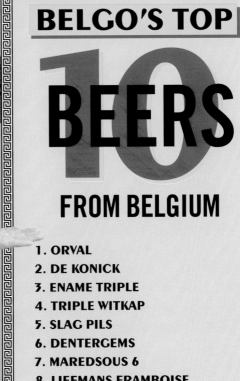

BELGO'S TOP
10
BEERS
FROM BELGIUM

1. ORVAL
2. DE KONICK
3. ENAME TRIPLE
4. TRIPLE WITKAP
5. SLAG PILS
6. DENTERGEMS
7. MAREDSOUS 6
8. LIEFMANS FRAMBOISE
9. CHIMAY GRANDE RESERVE
10. SIXTUS 8

WHITE BEERS

WHITE BEER, known to Belgians as witbier or bière blanche, is so-called because of its distinctive cloudy white appearance, caused by the yeast sediment mixing with the beer. The type of yeast used adds a refreshing lemony tartness. If it were poured too gently from the bottle it would look like a golden lager, but the yeast sediment is what gives white beer its characteristic colour and flavour. At Belgo we recommend Hoegaarden on tap, which we reckon gives the best mix of beer and yeast.

White beer is sometimes known as wheat beer: it is brewed from a mixture of malted barley and unmalted wheat (unlike German wheat beers, which use 100% malted grains), to which herbs and spices may be added, such as coriander and curaçao orange peels.

It is traditional to the eastern part of Belgium, around Leuven, a rural area where a lot of wheat is grown. The spices may sound surprising, but they're not really. In the 18thcentury, Belgium's Dutch neighbours, who had a great navy and colonies in the Far East, were well known for spice trading, and herbs and spices were used to flavour beer long before hops.

This style of beer had almost died out until it was revived in the 1960s by Pierre Celis at his brewery in the small town of Hoegaarden. White beer became so popular that it was soon being made by other breweries all over Belgium. The Hoegaarden brewery was eventually taken over by a much larger company and Pierre Celis moved to America — we hear that Belgian-style white beers are rapidly gaining fans in the States.

Light in colour and alcohol, this refreshingly tart, fruity beer is often drunk as an aperitif, sometimes with a slice of lemon to enhance the tartness. It is excellent to accompany fish and shellfish and is used a lot in cooking because it is aromatic and fruity, without any hoppy bitterness. Try adding a splash to sauerkraut just before serving.

Blanche de Namur
4.5% Spicy and slightly bitter.

Dentergems Witbier
5% Dry and refreshing, less spiced than other white beers.

Florisgaarden wit
5% Spritzy and slightly sour.

Hoegaarden Blanche
5% The classic of the style: tart, fruity and refreshing cloudy white beer, brewed with coriander and curaçao orange peels.

Titje
5% Light and fruity.

Vlaamsch Wit/ Blanche des Flandres (Flemish white)
4.5% Sweetish, fruity and slightly smoky.

FRUIT BEERS

I N THE AREA around Brussels, there is a long tradition of a Sunday afternoon family walk, ending at the pub. The men would order lambic or gueuze (see page 56), but these on their own were considered too sour for women. Instead they could be sweetened with sugar or grenadine, or flavoured with fruit. The locally grown fruit would have been either the rather sour, dark red variety of cherry known as kriek, or raspberries (framboise in French, frambozen in Flemish).

The traditional method was to macerate the whole fruit in lambic beer, which gave it a deep red colour. However, it is now commonplace - and far easier for large-scale brewers - to use a mixture of fruits and juices, or essences, to achieve a sweeter, more aromatic flavour.

Kriek and framboise beers were dying out in the 1960s and 1970s, when they were still considered 'women's drinks'. Their fortunes were revived when other fruit beers - low in alcohol, sweet and easy to drink - appeared on the market and a wider public rediscovered the originals. Peach and blackcurrant were the earliest of the new fruit beers, but there is now scarcely a fruit that has not been used to flavour beer.

Not all fruit beers are based on lambic. Flemish brown ales (see page 68) and white beers (see page 58) are also used.

In the pubs around Brussels, the traditional snack to go with lambic and gueuze-type beers is *plattekaas*, a slightly acidic soft white cheese. It is served with bread and, usually, radishes, although sometimes a sprinkling of cassonnade (soft brown sugar) replaces the radishes.

Fruit beers make wonderful aperitifs, especially if served in Champagne glasses. They are naturals with, or as an ingredient in, desserts, but in fact they work well as an ingredient in many dishes, because the acidity of the lambic-based beers cuts cleanly through heavy sauces. For the same reason they are a good choice after a huge, Belgo-style meal; light, refreshing and sourish, they take the place of a sorbet.

Belle-vue Frambozen
5.4% Sweet raspberry taste and syrupy aroma.

Belle-vue Kriek
5.2% Light-bodied, with cherry fruitiness.

Chapeau Banana, Strawberry, Pineapple or Plum Lambic
3% Sweet and light fruit-flavoured beers.

Florisgaarden Ninkeberry
3% White beer base with mangoes and apricots, very sweet.

Liefmans Frambozen
5.2% Flemish brown ale with raspberries, very aromatic.

Liefmans Kriek
6.5% Flemish brown ale with cherries, sweet and fruity.

Liefmans Gluhkriek
6.5% Belgium's answer to mulled wine. Cherry and spice flavoured, best served warm with a cinnamon stick.

St Louis Cassis
4.5% Like a Kir Royale, but based on Belgian beer, not French wine. Sweet blackcurrant aroma and sourish flavour.

St Louis Pêche
3.5% Full of peachy fruit flavour, light, sweet/sour.

TRAPPIST BEERS

NLY A BREW made at a Trappist monastery can use the word Trappist on its label. It is an appellation of origin, though not of style, since the monasteries are dotted around Belgium, and the beers come in a variety of colours and strengths. However, all the beers are strong in alcohol, top-fermented (in other words they use an ale yeast) and bottle-conditioned, with plenty of yeast sediment and a fruity, aromatic flavour.

The Trappist order is one of the strictest, with closed communities where women may not enter. There are five Trappist monasteries in Belgium: Orval, Chimay, Rochefort, Westmalle and Westvleteren. Westvleteren is not as commercial as the others, and its beers, sold as Sixtus, are notoriously difficult to get hold of, unless you happen to live near the monastery. The only other Trappist brewery in the world is Schaapskooi in the Netherlands.

Although the Trappist monasteries have long historical links (Orval was founded in the 12th century and Rochefort in the 13th), the ales were mainly developed in the 19th century, and Orval's beer was first brewed in 1931.

With the exception of Orval, each of the Trappist breweries has a beer that is dark brown, rich and sweetish: this style is sometimes known as double or dubbel. These are definitely the beers to go with game, red meat and winter casseroles. They are sometimes used to cook mussels and rabbit, in which case they can accompany the dish. The paler beers are mostly too strong to drink as aperitifs, but can be served with seafood. The strongest Trappist beers are good with strong cheeses and perfect as after-dinner drinks.

To appreciate the wonderfully complex aromas and flavours, these beers should be drunk at room temperature: about 12–16°C / 54–60°F.

Chimay Rouge

7% Dark, very fruity and yeasty, with something of a sweet/sour character.

Chimay Blonde

8% Pale, dry, hoppy and fruity.

Chimay Bleue

9% Dark, fruity and spicy - huge character.

Chimay Grande Reserve

9% Vintage Chimay Bleue served in a Champagne-corked bottle. The beer writer Michael Jackson has suggested this is the ideal accompaniment to Roquefort or Stilton cheese.

Orval

6.2% Amber-coloured, very dry with a bitter orange aroma and flavour. Its hop character makes it an excellent aperitif, and it is also good with fish and with Belgo's ragout de champignons, made with Orval beer and Orval cheese .

Rochefort 6

6 7.5% Dark amber to brown, fruity, with some unusual yeasty flavours.

Rochefort 8

9% Tawny-brown, rich and fruity.

Rochefort 10

11.3% Dark, powerful, sweet, with notes of bitter chocolate. This could be served as a dessert beer with a dessert of Belgian chocolate.

Sixtus 8

10% The beer made at Westvleteren abbey is, on rare occasions, available in London. This is one of our favourite beers: it's one of the most full-bodied beers you will ever taste, with the bitterness and slight sweetness of dark chocolate. It is almost a meal in itself, but is not overwhelming – the perfect drink for a cold winter night.

Westmalle Dubbel

6% Dark, soft and malty, with a hint of spiciness.

Westmalle Tripel

8% A world classic - golden, strong, with a huge complexity of flavours. It is good with seafood, and is the perfect accompaniment to the plump white best Belgian asparagus.

How does a Belgian tie his shoelace?

BROUWERIJ
DE KLUIS
HOEGAARDEN

ABBEY BEERS

THERE ARE SEVERAL MONASTERIES in Belgium that are not of the Trappist order, but none of them has made beer for many years. However, several of them license commercial breweries to produce beers for them. Most of these beers are similar in style to the Trappist beers (see previous page). Other breweries make beers that hint at a religious connection, perhaps with labels showing abbeys or monks. None of these beers can use the word Trappist and should be labelled with the word abbey (*abbaye* in French, *abdij* in Flemish).

Belgium has hundreds of these beers, in very varying styles (and quality); obviously we at Belgo have selected the best. Like the Trappist ales, abbey beers are strong and top-fermented; some are of an almost unbearable potency and sweetness.

Affligem Triple

8.5% Golden, malty, sweet and full.

Augustine

8% Deep amber, malty and clean taste.

Bornem Tripel

9% Golden, with a sweet malty aroma, full body and bitter aftertaste.

Brugse Tripel

9.5% Deep golden with a malty aroma; strong, full-bodied and sweet.

Corsendonk Agnus

8% Blond, fruity and slightly bitter.

Corsendonk Pater

8% Dark, with dark caramel sweetness.

Ename Double

6.5% Dark, sweet and malty.

Ename Triple

9% Golden, spicy and bitter.

Floreffe Tripel

8% Golden, strong and full, with a sweetish aroma and bitter aftertaste. Floreffe is an abbey near Namur; its beers are made by one of Belgium's best small breweries.

Het Kapitel Abt

10% Very full-bodied beer, with a tanginess characteristic of its brewery.

Het Kapitel Pater

6.5% The lightest beer in this range; dark, tangy with hints of sweetness.

Het Kapitel Prior

9% Golden, sweet and sour.

Leffe Blonde

6.5% Pale, full-bodied, malty aroma, dry, fruity taste.

Leffe Brune

6.3% Brown, full-flavoured, soft, fluffy, creamy and bitter-sweet.

Maredsous

6% (draught), 6.8% (in 33cl bottle) Amber-coloured and well-balanced, with a delicate floral-fruity perfume and soft, clean malt character. Made for the Benedictine abbey of Maredsous at Anhée-Denée, south of Namur.

Moinette Blonde

8.5% Spicy and full-bodied, with a citrus aroma and very complex, sweet-sour and bitter flavour.

Postel Double

7% Dark, rich and chocolatey.

St Benoit Brune

6.5% Dark, strong and sweet.

Steenbrugge Double

6.5% Dark and sweet.

Triple Moine

8% Golden, full, strong and malty.

Witkap Double

7% Dark, light and sweetish.

Witkap Stimulo

6% Pale and light-bodied, yet full of flavour, with a powerful, fruity aroma.

Witkap Tripel

7.5% Golden, strong, full-bodied, with a fruity aroma and bitter aftertaste.

PALE ALES

LIKE ENGLISH 'PALE ALES', these are copper-coloured, top-fermented beers, but don't compare the Belgian brews to the English! Belgian beers have a distinctive malt character and yeasty fruitiness, and are usually more carbonated and spritzy, and spicily, rather than hoppily, aromatic. In some pubs you can add even more yeast to enhance the flavour. In Belgium, each of the main brands keeps within its territory: De Koninck in and around Antwerp, Straffe Hendrik in Bruges.

They are very easy-drinking beers, on their own, with a bowl of frites and steak tartare (the classic partners in Antwerp), or with fried fish.

Artevelde
5.7% Light and sweetish, with a bitter finish.

De Koninck
5% (draught or bottled)
A classic, rounded, malty ale.

De Koninck Cuvée
7.7% Originally a commemorative beer brewed for Antwerp '93 (Antwerp's year as European city of culture). Slightly sweeter than the regular version.

Speciale Op-ale
5% Malty, fruity and slightly sweet beer with a big head of white foam. Made by De Smedt in the town of Opwijk, north-west of Brussels.

Straffe Hendrik
6% Pale golden colour, wheaty aroma, light-bodied, slightly sweet and tangy with a bitter finish.

Vieux Temps
5.5% ("Old Times") The most popular ale in Wallonia and widely available in Brussels, fruity and yeasty.

SEASONAL BEERS (SAISONS)

TRADITIONAL TO THE PROVINCE of Hainaut in southern Belgium (Wallonia), a very agricultural area, saisons (seasons) were made by farmer-brewers in the late autumn and winter when there was less farm work. In the days before refrigeration this was also the best time of year for brewing: in hot weather the fermenting beer would spoil. The beers were intended to be drunk in the fields in the following spring and summer. Saisons therefore have to be strong enough to last the season yet light enough to be quenching.

It is a very old style and is not always to modern taste. The beers were partly fermented in wooden casks and may have begun to oxidize, giving a strange, almost "off" flavour which is characteristic of the style. Other weird, yet wonderful, flavours came from small proportions of spelt (a type of wheat), large amounts of hops to preserve the beer, and often a handful of spices for good measure.

Saisons remain a very refreshing style of beer and are very good with basic rustic food, from charcuterie to sauerkraut and stews of beef, pork or lamb with potatoes or cabbage.

Belgo Blonde

5.5% Organic beer brewed in Belgium by Dupont. Spicy, hoppy aroma, with a light, pleasant bitterness in the finish.

Dupont

6.5% Classic beer from a classic brewery, aromatic and spicy.

Pipaix

6.5% Very aromatic, spicy, tart and dry.

Saison Silly

5% Light and refreshing, traditional Wallonian beer.

WINE BEERS (RED BEERS)

FLEMISH BROWN ALES (OUD BRUIN)

VELVETY SMOOTH, with a burnt aroma, red beers, a regional speciality of West Flanders, are known as the Burgundies of Belgium. The clear, wine-like colour is derived from a particular type of barley and malt, as well as from the tannins and caramels extracted from the Polish oak casks in which the beers mature.

The beers have an oaky quality, and a peculiar, even vinegary, sourness deriving from bacteria that live in the wood casks. Some people don't like this sourness, but others love it, and find it a most refreshing, summery beer. Some drinkers add grenadine syrup to soften the tartness.

Rodenbach, made in Roeselare, is the classic example, and in its home province of West Flanders there is a delightful custom of buying a bag of brown shrimps from the fishmonger, then going to the pub and ordering a Rodenbach to drink with the shrimps.

These are excellent aperitif beers and are very useful in cooking. They are also good as an accompaniment to sweetish stews such as rabbit in kriek (see page 82) or dishes cooked in Trappist ale; the red beer gives a delicious sweet-sour effect.

Bacchus
4.5% Fruity and lactic aroma; sweet and sour taste.

Rodenbach Grand Cru
6.5% Fruity and oaky, with a sweet aroma and refreshingly sour taste.

TRADITIONAL TO EAST FLANDERS, "Old brown" ales, are generally reddish brown and have a distinctive sourish flavour. These characteristics are a result of several factors: dark malts and roasted grains are boiled for a long time, giving a hint of caramelization; the region's water is high in sodium bicarbonate; and beer-friendly bacteria live in the wooden maturation casks.

The classic of the style was Liefmans Goudenband, originally made in the town of Oudenaarde. With commercialization it lost a lot of its sourness and it has become a sweeter beer. While the original sourish style was the perfect partner to rustic meat dishes and stews, the more commercial sweeter style is often great with chocolate.

Bios Vlaamse Bourgogne
6% ('Flemish Burgundy') Light, sourish and slightly fruity.

Liefmans Goudenband
8% Although now leaning to the sweet rather than the sour, this is still a world-class ale.

Liefmans Oud Bruin
5% Sweet and very smooth.

Gouden Carolus
7.5% An excellent after-dinner drink, rich, sweet and full. Malty aroma, lightly hoppy, with a creamy texture.

Roman Special
5.5% Mellow and slightly bitter.

GOLDEN ALES

ALTHOUGH SIMILAR to lager in colour, Belgian golden ales are strong, aromatic and full of fruit and hops. Their alcoholic complexity is often developed through an elaborate triple fermentation process.

The original of the style is Duvel, made by Moortgat. It was once a dark strong ale, in imitation of the Scotch ales that became popular in Belgium after the First World War, but in 1968 the brewery created a golden version that was as tempting as the devil (duvel in a Flemish dialect). Its many imitators acknowledge the original in their choice of name.

These golden ales should be served quite cold. Because of their strength they are best enjoyed as a drink on their own. If you feel you need food to avoid a knock-out effect, try them with mussels or an eel dish.

Delirium Tremens
9% Malty aroma, full and sweet with a bitter finish.

Duvel
8.5% Strong and malty, with a bitter hop aftertaste.

Lucifer
8% Full-bodied with a citrus and wheat aroma and bitter finish.

Piraat
10.5% ("Pirate") Malty and very strong.

Sloeber
7.5% ("Joker") Full and strong, extra smooth with a malty aroma.

SPECIALITY BEERS

These are some of Belgium's regional specialities that are difficult to place within any category; their colours, strengths, styles and tastes are unique.

Affligem Noel

7% Dark, rich and chocolatey.

Arabier

8% Pale amber with a hoppy aroma and a bitter aftertaste.

Barbar

8% Strong amber ale brewed with honey, giving a slightly sweet flavour.

Brigand

9% Strong, dark amber-coloured, full-bodied and malty.

Bush

12% Belgium's strongest ale, similar to Britain's barley wine but - we think - easier to drink.

Campus Amber

7% Amber-coloured, sweetish ale.

Campus Gold

6% Blonde, malty and sweetish.

Chateau des Flandres

8% Dark, bitter-sweet and spicy.

Dikkenek

5% Dark ale brewed with juniper berries.

Dupont Xmas

9.5% Well-made, full-bodied, dark spicy ale.

Flierefluiter

7% Blonde, full-bodied and sweetish; slightly bitter finish.

Gordon Christmas

8.8% Dark, strong and warming. Brewed in Belgium but based on Scottish "heavy" ale.

Green Dragon

5.5% Bright green! A blend of 17 herbs is used in making this beer.

Hoegaarden Grand Cru

8.7% Pale golden with a honey aroma and taste. It is not a wheat beer, but is seasoned with coriander and curacao orange peels.

Julius

8.8% Golden ale with a green apple aroma.

Kasteel

11% ("Castle") Strong, slightly fruity, very warming to sip.

La Divine

9.5% Amber, strong, full, bitter-sweet and spicy.

La Gauloise Brune

9% Dark, strong and chocolatey.

McGregor

6.5% Dark, sweet and smoky. Uses peat-smoked malts, like those used in whisky-making.

Oerbier

7% Dark, smooth, creamy and sweet with hints of ripe strawberries.

Pauwel Kwak

8% Dark, full and warming with a light liquorice taste. Served in its specially designed miniature "yard of ale" glass.

Poperings Hommelbier

7.5% (Hop-beer) Amber-coloured, strong, creamy, spicy and very hoppy.

Scotch Silly

8% Strong Scotch-style ale: reddish-brown, sweet and nutty, full-bodied, warming and superbly rounded.

Verboden Vrucht

9% (Forbidden Fruit) Strong, dark, rich and complex, with sweet, spicy and fruity flavours; surprisingly easy drinking.

PILSNERS

THE WORLD'S FIRST clear golden beer was brewed in 1842 in Pilsen, Bohemia (now part of the Czech Republic). At about the same time, mass-produced glassware was replacing stone drinking vessels. The world could see how good this beer was, and almost immediately began to copy the technique. Every country has its golden lagers, and Belgium is no exception, although Belgium, with its enormous choice of individual ales, held out against the Pilsner invasion until the 1920s.

When Belgian brewers started to make Pilsners, they made them well. They are golden coloured with a high hop content, which gives the beer a good bite, delicate hop aroma and elegant hoppy dryness of flavour.

Bel Pils
5.3% Bavarian-style Pilsner with a great hop character.

Jupiler
5.2% Belgium's No 1-selling beer.

Riva Pils
5% Light with a sweet aroma and slightly bitter aftertaste.

Slag Lager
4.8% Light, hoppy and fruity; matured in the traditional way, for sixty days. The name derives from the brewery that makes it, Slaghmuylder.

La Cuisine
à la Bière

BEER IS TO THE BELGIANS what wine is to the French and Italians. In fact, it is a whole lot more than that. The English associate Belgium mainly with chocolates and the motorway route to their true Euro destination (although hopefully, Belgo has helped to change this image). But to the rest of Europe, Belgium means *moules*, *frites* and *bière*... glorious beer.

One of the most important aspects that distinguishes French *cuisine du terroir* from the Belgian repertoire is that Belgians cook and marinate a great deal with their fabulous beers. *Lapin à la kriek* (rabbit cooked in cherry beer), *pintadeau à la framboise* (guinea fowl in raspberry beer), *huîtres à la gueuze* (oysters in sweet sour beer), *carbonade flamande* (beef stewed in fruit and beer) – these are just a few of the more popular dishes in Belgian beer cookery.

ALLEZ - LET'S GO!

Denis and André's
GUIDE TO COOKING WITH BEER

1 In making the marinade, make sure you pour enough beer to cover the meat.

2 Leave meat to marinate 24–28 hours, enough time for a long poker game.

3 Use your beer marinade to cook the meat...very slowly.

4 You should reduce your beer marinade by one third nearing the end of cooking.

5 (Above) Add a final glass of beer a few minutes before serving.

6 (Below) Serve meat on plate, pouring beer sauce to cover. Serve with appropriate beer, if there's any left.

LA CUISINE À LA BIÈRE

SOUPE À LA BIÈRE (BEER SOUP)

BREWING IN BELGIUM dates back to when the Gauls were bashing up those poor Roman soldiers. In those days they used to drink an alcoholic cereal concoction called *cervoise*. Although brewing never really reached its full popularity in the Lowlands until the 16th century, its reputation was of the highest, and certainly the locals were using beer to cook with before that time.

When brewing finally made its mark, beer replaced wine-drinking on a large scale. The Franks, the French Burgundian Court and the Spanish all brought their wines and wine-making methods into Belgium and made it the official drink of the Courts. But civil wars and religious battles combined with a series of long winters put local brewers under pressure.

Dishes like *carbonade flamande* date back to medieval times. The beef was originally cooked with water, onions and thyme. Onions from Flanders were sought after by all of Europe because of their size and sweetness. Although wine was probably used in cooking until it became unobtainable, beer, with its very earthy taste, lent itself very well to the stewing of beef. It also proved a better tenderizer than wine. Most of the ancient Belgian dishes were the result of little accidents or folkloric experiments: people using whatever they had, and what was considered good, to cook with. Recipes were passed on as family traditions and rarely written down.

The addition of fruit, such as apples and plums, in cookery came later to enhance taste. It took away some of the bitterness that would come from using the strong local beer. *Cassonade* (brown sugar) or a sweet *pain d'épices* (gingerbread loaf) was sometimes used instead of fruit to both thicken and sweeten at the same time. Some used a slice of brown bread spread with mustard to enhance a dish.

The true *cuisine à la bière* really took off in the mid-19th century with the boom of Belgian brewers and the creation of

SERVES 4
50 g / 2 oz butter
400 g / 14 oz potatoes, roughly chopped
1 leek, roughly chopped
1 onion, chopped
500 ml / 16 fl oz Hoegaarden white beer
1 bayleaf and 1 sprig of thyme, tied together
salt and pepper

Melt the butter in a large saucepan, add the chopped potatoes, leek and onion and cook over a low heat for 5 minutes.

Add the beer and 1 litre / 1¾ pints water, the herbs and seasoning and simmer for 1 hour.

Remove the bunch of herbs, then pass the soup through a vegetable mill or blend in a liquidizer. Reheat and serve hot.

speciality beers such as *kriek* (cherry beer) and *gueuze* (a sparkling sour beer). Dishes like *lapin à la kriek* (rabbit in cherry beer) became famous and took their place in the Belgian *repertoire de cuisine*.

Cuisine à la bière is a tradition of using beer as a marinade, sauce base or as a flavouring. The variety of Belgian beers, which are so distinctive in taste and character, lend themselves perfectly to this concept of cooking. Today this method is more popular than ever and it has been further enhanced by the inspiration of Belgium's eccentric brewers. It is only a matter of time before *cuisine à la bière* finds its well-deserved permanent place on the menus of the world's best tables.

Huîtres à la gueuze
(Oysters in sour beer)

SERVES 2

2 small carrots

2 thin leeks

125 g / 4 oz peeled celeriac

salt

12 oysters

3 egg yolks

200 ml / 7 fl oz gueuze beer

Cut the carrots, leeks and celeriac into very fine strips. Blanch each vegetable separately in salted boiling water for 2-3 minutes, then drain and refresh under cold running water to set the colour.

Preheat the grill.

Protect your hands with thick tea towels as you open the oysters. Grip each oyster firmly in your palm and keep it level so you do not lose the juice. Insert the tip of your oyster knife into the crack near the hinge of the oyster. Force the knife in and twist to sever the nerve and open the shell. Cut the oyster away from the top and bottom of the shell, then tip the oyster and its juice into a small saucepan. When you have opened all the oysters, poach them in their juice for 1 minute. Remove from the heat and set aside.

Put the egg yolks in a saucepan over a very low heat and gradually whisk in the beer. Keep whisking until the sauce thickens, then remove from the heat.

Divide the vegetable strips between two small gratin dishes. Using a slotted spoon, lift the oysters out of their juice and place on top of the vegetables. Pour over the beer sauce and put the dishes under the hot grill for 30 seconds, until the sauce is beginning to turn golden brown. Serve at once.

Lotte à la kriek et
aux petits légumes
(Monkfish with cherry beer
and baby vegetables)

SERVES 4

12 baby fennel bulbs

12 baby carrots

12 baby turnips

12 pencil-thin leeks

100 ml / 3½ fl oz fish stock

1 bottle (25 cl) kriek / cherry beer

2 bay leaves

2–3 sprigs of thyme

salt and pepper

675 g / 1½ lb monkfish fillets,
     cut into 2.5 cm / 1 inch thick slices

85 ml / 3 fl oz cherry purée

100 ml / 3½ fl oz double cream

Cook the baby vegetables in salted boiling water until just tender, then drain and refresh under cold running water. Set aside.

Put the fish stock and beer in a saucepan, bring to the boil and simmer for 10 minutes to reduce the liquid.

Fill a wide saucepan with water, add the bay leaves, thyme and a pinch of salt. Bring to the boil, then add the monkfish and simmer gently for 5 minutes. Remove the pan from the heat and lift the fish out of the beer, using a slotted spoon.

Add the cherry purée and cream to the beer sauce; season to taste and heat through gently.

Reheat the vegetables in a pan of boiling water.

Pour the sauce on to four warmed serving plates. Arrange the sliced monkfish in a circle in the centre of the plates, with the vegetables around the fish; serve at once.

Coucou de Malines à la Moinette
(Chicken with beer, cream and mustard sauce)

SERVES 2

1 poussin (young chicken), about 1 kg / 2¼ lb
salt and pepper
200 ml / 7 fl oz Moinette beer
250 ml / 8 fl oz double cream
2 teaspoons Dijon mustard

CELERIAC PURÉE

½ a celeriac root
25 g / 1 oz butter

Preheat the oven to 190° C / 375° F / Gas Mark 5.

Season the chicken inside and out and roast for about 45 minutes.

Peel and cube the celeriac, boil until tender, then drain and set aside, ready to purée.

Mix half the beer and half the cream with the mustard.

When the chicken is cooked, remove from the oven and leave to rest for 5 minutes, then cut in half and keep warm on a plate.

Purée the celeriac and reheat gently with the butter.

Pour the remaining beer into the roasting tin, place over medium heat and stir to deglaze and loosen the roasting residue. Bring to the boil, add the remaining cream and simmer for 2–3 minutes, whisking in the mustard mixture.

Serve the chicken on warmed plates, with the celeriac purée and the sauce poured over.

Canard à la bière cassis
(Duck with blackcurrant beer sauce)

SERVES 2

1 duck, quartered
400 g / 14 oz goose fat
200 ml / 7 fl oz duck stock
85 ml / 3 fl oz cassis / blackcurrant beer
50 g / 2 oz blackcurrants

Put the duck legs and goose fat into a shallow dish and leave to marinate for 24 hours.

Put the duck legs and goose fat into a saucepan and cook over a low heat for 1½ hours or until the meat is very tender.

Boil the duck stock over a high heat to reduce by half.

Meanwhile, heat a heavy-bottomed frying pan and fry the duck breasts over a high heat for about 10 minutes, turning occasionally, until just cooked.

When the stock has reduced to about 125 ml / 4 fl oz, add the beer and the blackcurrants.

Slice and fan the duck breasts and arrange on two serving plates with the duck legs. Pour the sauce around the duck. Serve with celeriac purée (see left) and deep-fried shredded celeriac.

Pintade à la framboise
(Guinea fowl in raspberry beer)

SERVES 2

50 g / 2 oz butter

1 guinea fowl

salt and pepper

½ large onion, roughly chopped

1 carrot, roughly chopped

1 bayleaf

1 sprig of thyme

1 bottle (25 cl) framboise / raspberry beer

100 ml / 3½ fl oz chicken stock

Preheat the oven to 190° C / 375° F / Gas Mark 5.

Melt the butter in a roasting tin over medium heat. Season the guinea fowl inside and out and brown on all sides in the roasting tin. Add the onion, carrot, bayleaf and thyme and roast in the oven for about 30 minutes.

Remove the guinea fowl from the tin and keep warm.

Pour the beer and stock into the roasting tin, place over medium heat and stir to deglaze and loosen the roasting residue. Bring to the boil and simmer for 10 minutes to reduce the liquid.

Strain the liquid through a conical sieve into a jug. Cut the guinea fowl in half and serve on warmed plates, with the sauce poured over. Serve with sauté potatoes or sauerkraut.

VARIATION

Faisan à la Rodenbach
(Pheasant in Rodenbach red ale)

Use pheasant instead of guinea fowl and replace the raspberry beer with Rodenbach red ale.

Lapin à la kriek
(Rabbit in cherry beer)

SERVES 4

2 rabbits

2 carrots, sliced

2 onions, sliced

2 bay leaves

10 peppercorns

1 bottle (25 cl) kriek / cherry beer

2 tablespoons flour

salt and pepper

2 tablespoons peanut oil

15 g / ½ oz butter

400 g / 14 oz pitted black cherries in natural juice

Cut the rabbits into pieces and use the trimmings to make stock, with 1 carrot, 1 onion, 1 bay leaf, 5 peppercorns and 600 ml / 1 pint water. Cover and simmer for about 1½ hours, then strain into a jug and reserve.

Marinate the rabbit pieces in the beer with the remaining carrot, onion, bay leaf and peppercorns for 24 hours. Using a slotted spoon, remove the rabbit from the marinade and pat dry. Coat the rabbit in seasoned flour. Heat the oil and butter in a sauté pan and fry the rabbit until lightly browned on all sides.

Reserve 32 of the black cherries and purée the remainder with a little of the juice.

Remove the saddle pieces and front legs from the pan and add 400 ml / 14 fl oz of the stock, together with the beer marinade and the puréed cherries. Simmer the back legs for about 20 minutes, then return the saddles and front legs to the pan. Taste and adjust the seasoning and simmer for a further 20–30 minutes, until the rabbit is tender.

To serve, stir in the reserved cherries with a little of their juice and serve at once, in a soup plate, with boiled potatoes.

Noisettes de chevreuil et poire pochée, sauce à la kriek Liefmans
(Noisettes of venison with poached pear and cherry beer sauce)

SERVES 4
2 pears
generous pinch of ground cinnamon
100 g / 3½ oz brown sugar
2 bottles (25 cl each) Liefmans Kriek / cherry beer
800 g / 1¾ lb venison steak
salt and pepper
40 g / 1½ oz butter
200 g / 7 oz cherries in syrup
200 ml / 7 fl oz venison (or veal) stock

Preheat the oven to 200° C / 400° F / Gas Mark 6.

Peel the pears, cut in half lengthways and place in a small saucepan with the cinnamon, sugar and beer. Simmer until the pears are tender, then remove the pan from the heat, leaving the pears in the liquid.

Season the venison. Heat the butter in a large frying pan and lightly brown the venison on both sides, then roast in the oven for 3–4 minutes, until the meat is tender but still pink in the centre.

Meanwhile, add half the pear cooking liquid, the cherries and the venison stock to the pan in which the venison was fried and simmer for 5–8 minutes.

To serve, slice the pears lengthways without cutting right through so that they can be fanned out at the top of each plate. Put the venison at the bottom of the plates and pour the sauce over it; serve at once.

Agneau à la Duvel et gratin dauphinois
(Lamb with Duvel beer and gratin dauphinois)

SERVES 4
800 g / 1¾ lb lamb steaks
salt and pepper
25 g / 1 oz butter
1 bottle (33 cl) Duvel strong golden ale
200 ml / 7 fl oz lamb stock

GRATIN DAUPHINOIS
4 large potatoes
2 garlic cloves, crushed
1 teaspoon chopped fresh thyme leaves
300 ml / ½ pint milk
200 ml / 7 fl oz double cream
freshly grated nutmeg

Preheat the oven to 190° C / 375° F / Gas Mark 5.

First make the gratin dauphinois. Slice the potatoes very thinly and place in an ovenproof dish. Add the garlic, thyme, milk, cream, nutmeg and seasoning, cover the dish and place in the oven for 45 minutes.

Season the lamb. Heat the butter in a large frying pan and brown the lamb on both sides, then finish cooking in the oven for 3–4 minutes.

Meanwhile, add the beer and stock to the frying pan and simmer gently for 10 minutes.

To serve, divide the potato gratin and lamb steaks between four serving plates and pour over the sauce; serve at once.

Foie de veau à la Rodenbach
(Calves' liver with Rodenbach red ale)

SERVES 4

85 g / 3 oz butter

2 red onions, thinly sliced

200 ml / 7 fl oz red wine

675 g / 1½ lb calves' liver, trimmed and thinly sliced

2 tablespoons flour

salt and pepper

1 bottle (25 cl) Rodenbach beer

300 ml / ½ pint veal stock

Melt half the butter in a saucepan and fry the onions for about 5 minutes, until softened but not browned. Add the red wine and simmer for 30–40 minutes, until very soft.

Coat the liver in seasoned flour. Heat the remaining butter in a large frying pan over medium-high heat and fry the liver for about 2 minutes on each side, until sealed but still pink in the centre. Remove from the pan and keep warm.

Pour the beer and stock into the pan and increase the heat to high. Stir to deglaze the pan and boil until the liquid has reduced and thickened.

Serve the liver on a bed of the red onion mixture, accompanied by stoemp (see page 108) and lentils, and pour the beer sauce over the liver.

Filet de porc à la Westmalle Dubbel
(Pork fillet with Westmalle Dubbel Trappist ale)

SERVES 4

85 g / 3 oz butter

4 potatoes (preferably Cara), cubed

100 g / 3½ oz Ardennes ham

675 g / 1½ lb pork fillet

1 bottle (33 cl) Westmalle Dubbel dark Trappist ale

200 ml / 7 fl oz double cream

salt and pepper

Preheat the oven to 190° C / 375° F / Gas Mark 5.

Melt the butter in a sauté pan and sauté the potatoes until lightly browned all over.

Cut the ham into thin strips and sauté with the potatoes for 1–2 minutes, then transfer to an ovenproof dish and bake in the oven for 20 minutes.

Meanwhile, trim the pork and cut into medallions. Season and fry until well browned, then place in the oven for about 8 minutes or until cooked. Remove from the oven and keep warm.

Pour the beer into the pan in which the pork was fried and simmer for 2 minutes, then add the cream and simmer for a further 1–2 minutes. Season to taste.

To serve, place the pork medallions on four serving plates and mound the potatoes on top. Pour the sauce over the meat and serve at once.

Rognons de veau à la Trappiste Chimay Rouge
(Calves' kidneys in Chimay Trappist beer sauce)

SERVES 4

800 g / 1¾lb calves' kidneys in their suet
4 tablespoons plain flour
salt and pepper
50 g / 2 oz butter
1 bottle (33 cl) Chimay Rouge beer
150 ml (¼ pint) veal stock

Cut the kidneys into 1 cm / ½ inch thick slices, leaving a thin layer of suet around the edge. Toss the kidneys in seasoned flour to coat them evenly. Melt the butter in a frying pan until it begins to foam, then add the kidneys and fry for 3 minutes on each side.

Remove the kidneys from the frying pan and keep warm. Pour the veal stock and three-quarters of the Chimay beer into the pan, bring to the boil and let it reduce to about 200 ml / 7 fl oz. Season to taste. Return the kidneys and any juices to the frying pan and heat for 1 minute. Add the remaining Chimay beer and cook for 30 seconds. Serve the kidneys on warmed plates and pour the beer sauce over the kidneys.

Carbonade flamande
(Flemish beef stew)

SERVES 6

1.5 kg / 3 lb chuck steak, cut into 5 cm / 2 inch chunks
700 ml / 1¼ pints Liefmans Goudenband
2 tablespoons peanut oil
25 g / 1 oz butter
25 g / 1 oz brown sugar
1 tablespoon freshly grated nutmeg
salt and pepper
3 tablespoons flour
2 tablespoons tomato purée
125 g / 4 oz pitted prunes, sliced
400 ml / 14 fl oz veal stock
1 bouquet garni
1–2 tablespoons Dijon mustard
2 cooking apples

Marinate the meat in 500 ml / ¾ pint of the beer for 3 days.

Lift the meat out of the marinade, reserving the marinade. Heat the oil and butter in a large, heavy-based frying pan, add the meat, sugar and nutmeg and cook over a medium-high heat, stirring frequently, until the meat is well browned. Using a slotted spoon, transfer the meat to a casserole and season with salt and pepper.

Stir the flour into the oil and butter and cook until well browned, then stir in the tomato purée, prunes, veal stock, bouquet garni and the beer marinade. Bring to the boil, skim and then pour over the meat. Simmer very gently until the meat is tender, about 1 hour.

Stir in the mustard and the remaining beer, then taste and adjust the seasoning. Peel and quarter the apples, add to the casserole and cook for 5–10 minutes, until the apples are tender. Serve hot.

Fruits marinés à la bière framboise
(Fruit salad with raspberry beer)

SERVES 4

1 apple

1 pear

400 ml / 14 fl oz framboise / raspberry beer

150 g / 5 oz caster sugar

8 mint leaves, shredded

12 strawberries

2 bananas

175 g / 6 oz raspberries

It is best to begin making this dish a day in advance. Peel the apple and pear and slice them thinly. Put them in a bowl with the beer, sugar and shredded mint leaves, cover and leave in the refrigerator overnight.

The following morning, slice the bananas into the bowl and add the raspberries and strawberries. Return to the refrigerator until ready to serve.

Serve the fruit and juices in glass bowls or soup plates, with fresh cream if desired.

Sorbets à la bière
(Fruit beer sorbets)

SERVES 4

200 g / 7 oz caster sugar

85 ml / 3 fl oz fruit beer (framboise / raspberry, kriek / cherry or pêche / peach)

100 ml / 3½ fl oz fruit purée or juice (raspberry, cherry or peach)

TO SERVE

150 ml / ¼ pint fruit purée

sprigs of mint

Put the sugar in a saucepan with 200 ml / 7 fl oz water and bring to the boil. Boil for 2 minutes, then leave to cool.

Mix the cold syrup with the beer and fruit purée and place it in an ice-cream maker to process. When the sorbet is firm, transfer it to a freezer container and freeze until required.

To serve, scoop two or three balls of sorbet into each serving bowl and serve with a few tablespoons of fruit purée and a sprig of mint.

Traditional
Belgian dishes

WHEN IT COMES TO their own home cooking, the Belgians have tended to remain purists and have kept their cuisine too much to themselves. This probably stems from years of foreign rule on their home turf. With the rise of Flemish and Walloon nationalism in the seventies, Belgian traditional cooking got the opportunity to raise its regional flags alongside the resurgence of traditional beers. Grandmothers' dishes started to appear not only in popular student cafés but also in all the fashionable restaurants across Belgium.

ALLEZ…ENJOY!

ONE OF BELGIUM's most fashionable restaurants is the Brabançon in the Rue de la Commune in Brussels. This establishment managed to survive the hedonistic eighties, when everything new came in and everything old went out. It remained true to a cuisine that was almost forgotten by the new influx of restaurant-goers. Unfortunately the décor has not kept up with time, but in our eyes that makes it even more fun. Marie-Jeanne Lucas, proprietor and head chef at the Brabançon, is not too bothered about changing the style of the place: she was awarded the Grand Prix de la Cuisine Artisanale et Régionale. She has also just celebrated her 77th birthday!

Belgo owes much to Marie-Jeanne's time and kindness in sharing her secrets and passion for Belgian traditional cooking. Never mind the rather peculiar paintings of horses labouring the fields that dominate the walls of her restaurant. Never mind the three pug dogs and Titje the parrot. The main reason you are at the Brabançon is to taste true Belgian cuisine in its purist form. When Madame Lucas serves you your pound of butter with a knife stuck through it you know you're in the right place.

Nowadays many restaurants in Belgium have started to acknowledge that their national cuisine deserves wider recognition and a better place than on the menus of tourist traps. Yes – now even the fashion-conscious Belgians themselves would like to sample some of grandmother's deliciously prepared dishes in less intimate environments than their own homes. The Spinnenkopke, which specializes in *cuisine à la bière*, Le Canterbury and Le Petit Pont restaurants in Brussels are all fine examples of this new wave of *la cuisine traditionnelle Belge*.

At times Belgo has been heralded as the true Belgian Embassy in London for its role in promoting Belgian cuisine and beers and in doing so promoting Belgian culture itself. Of course we are very grateful for all the recognition we have received from some of the most widely read Belgian newspapers and magazines, but even more so we are now glad to be just a few minutes away from a *tomates crevettes* or *witloof au gratin*. We hope the following recipes will save you a few ferry tickets but not stop you from visiting Belgo.

TYPICAL BELGIAN INGREDIENTS

The most satisfying thing about producing the food for the menus at Belgo is that we do not need to bring our ingredients from far and exotic places. Well, one could consider the Outer Hebrides somewhat exotic, but generally nothing comes further than from Belgium or Holland. The true beauty of Belgian food is its sublime simplicity.

The ingredients that are used for the recipes at Belgo are typical of those used in traditional Belgian dishes, such as *waterzooi* and *carbonade*. We remain true to the traditional recipes, though we may vary the amount of fat and butter that was once used. Belgians were so renowned for the amount of butter they consumed that the government recently issued a warning asking restaurants not to serve dishes such as *raie au beurre noir* (skate cooked in *beurre noisette*), so heavy with butter, because of concern about the Belgian population's cardiac problems. (This problem was originally recorded by one of François I's doctors, who referred to the Belgians as a bunch of *bouffeurs de beurre* or butter eaters.)

We felt confident that Belgo would succeed because we knew that our guests would feel extremely familiar with ingredients such as leeks, asparagus, potatoes, beetroot, carrots, fennel, onion, celery, thyme, chives, rosemary, turnips, radish, beef, chicken, fish, butter and cream to name but a few. They sound so familiar you would think your grandmother had just opened up a restaurant. It is not so much where and how far you get your ingredients from that is important. Rather it is their freshness and what one does with them that is the substance of making good food.

It's important to note that, since the 14th century, Belgium, together with Holland, has been the "vegetable basket" of Europe. Together the two countries were the first to mass produce and export fresh vegetables. Today they export the largest volume of vegetables in Europe.

Britain owes much to Belgium for the introduction of new vegetables. It was after all Belgians from Flanders who introduced the carrot and the turnip to Britain. And the potato was first exported to Britain back in the mid-18th century. Belgium was also responsible for developing many new types of vegetables such as the Brussels sprout, the witloof (chicory or Belgian endive) and hop shoots.

Nowadays the witloof is omnipresent in Belgian cooking. At Belgo we use it for salads, soups, garnish, puréed, and as a cooked vegetable. The Belgians regard the witloof as their most treasured vegetable. Even the *choux de Bruxelles* can not match it on presence and recognition. Witloof, braised in butter with a dash of lemon, brown sugar and nutmeg is bliss! *Witloof au gratin* (braised chicory wrapped with ham in bechamel sauce and then gratinéed) is a Belgo top seller.

The leek also holds a particularly high place in the Belgian repertoire. Similar to the endive and a great alternative to the more expensive asparagus, it is used at Belgo in all our vegetable *julienne* and to flavour our fish as in the *waterzooi de poisson*.

Nutmeg is probably the most important spice in Belgian cuisine. It is used as seasoning rather like pepper, sprinkled on butter-fried vegetables and also to flavour *stoemp* (Belgian mashed potato with cooked vegetables; similar to bubble'n'squeak). *Stoemp* is super. You will find it on any simple traditional Belgian restaurant's menu. It accompanies sausages and meats very well.

Asparagus has been part of the Belgian family meal since the 16th century. Every year in May the white asparagus season starts and in Belgium, Germany and Holland this is celebrated with great relish. You can stroll into any local restaurant and find that special menus have been set out featuring the white asparagus as a starter or for main course portions. Some restaurants specializing in mussels will use the occasion to replace the seasonal shellfish in this period with asparagus. The white asparagus from Malines is the best you can get. At Belgo we make sure we have both year round by using green asparagus when the white season ends. You can serve asparagus with almost any sauce. The most typical Belgian way of eating asparagus is steamed, and then cooked in butter with hard-boiled egg and chives.

Tomates farcies de crevettes grises
(Tomatoes stuffed with shrimps and mayonnaise)

SERVES 2
4 tomatoes
1 large bunch of lambs' lettuce (corn salad)
200 g / 7 oz peeled brown shrimps
1 tablespoon chopped fresh chives
100 ml / 3½ fl oz mayonnaise
4 tablespoons vinaigrette dressing

Bring a saucepan of water to the boil. Using a sharp knife, mark a cross on the base of each tomato, then place in the boiling water for 10 seconds. Remove from the water and refresh under cold running water. Peel the tomatoes, then slice off their tops and scoop out the seeds and pulp.

Wash and drain the lambs' lettuce.

Mix the shrimps with the chives and pack about half of them into the tomatoes. Put the tomatoes on two serving plates and top with mayonnaise. Toss the corn salad in vinaigrette and arrange it around the stuffed tomatoes, with the remaining shrimps. Garnish with half a lemon.

Crème de chicons à la bière blanche
(Cream of chicory soup with wheat beer)

SERVES 4
4 heads of chicory
50 g / 2 oz butter
1 small onion, thinly sliced
4 large potatoes, quartered
50 g / 2 oz brown sugar
1 bouquet garni
300 ml / ½ pint white beer
1 litre / 1¾ pints chicken stock or water
salt and pepper
freshly grated nutmeg
250 ml / 8 fl oz double cream

Cut the chicory in half lengthways and cut out the cores. Slice the chicory thinly. Melt the butter in a saucepan, add the onion and cook for 1 minute. Add the chicory, potatoes, sugar and bouquet garni and cook over a low heat for 15 minutes.

Add the beer, stock or water, salt, pepper and nutmeg. Simmer gently for about 1 hour.

Remove the bouquet garni and blend the soup in a liquidizer or pass it through a food mill. Return the soup to the saucepan, add the cream and bring back to the boil. Taste and adjust the seasoning if necessary; serve hot.

Coquilles oostendaise
(Scallops with seafood and cream sauce)

SERVES 4

85 g / 3 oz celeriac

2 small carrots

1 leek

50 g / 2 oz butter

8-12 scallops, with 4 shells

3 tablespoons white beer

100 ml / 3½ fl oz double cream

8–12 mussels, freshly cooked

85 g / 3 oz peeled brown shrimps

salt and pepper

Peel the celeriac and carrots and trim the leek. Cut all the vegetables into very fine (julienne) strips. Melt the butter in a saucepan, add the vegetables and cook over a low heat until they are just tender, but still quite crisp to the bite. Remove and set aside.

Cut the scallops horizontally into three or four slices (depending on their size). Heat a nonstick frying pan and add the scallops; cook for 30 seconds on each side. Remove from the pan and set aside.

Heat the beer in a saucepan over a low heat for 2 minutes, then add the cream, mussels, shrimps and seasoning, and cook for a further 2 minutes.

To serve, preheat the grill. Divide the vegetables between four scallop shells and place the scallops on top. Pour the sauce over and place under the hot grill for 30 seconds. Serve at once, with lemon wedges.

Toast cannibale
(Steak tartare crostini)

SERVES 1

100 g / 3½ oz beef fillet

25 g / 1 oz gherkins, finely chopped

25 g / 1 oz shallots, finely chopped

25 g / 1 oz capers, chopped

1 drop of Tabasco sauce

1 tablespoon mayonnaise

salt and pepper

2 slices of French bread

Finely mince the beef and mix with the chopped gherkins, shallots, capers, Tabasco, mayonnaise and seasoning to taste.

Lightly toast the French bread and spread the beef mixture over the bread. If you like, serve with salad leaves, gherkins and pickled onions.

CROQUETTES DE FROMAGE
(CHEESE CROQUETTES)

SERVES 4

3 gelatine leaves
300 ml / ½ pint milk
50 g / 2 oz butter
150 g / 5 oz plain flour
100 g / 3½ oz Gruyère cheese, grated
100 g / 3½ oz Cheddar cheese, grated
salt and pepper
freshly grated nutmeg
150 g / 5 oz breadcrumbs
2 eggs
vegetable oil for deep-frying
bunch of curly parsley

Soak the gelatine leaves in cold water until they are soft. Heat the milk in a saucepan, then add the softened gelatine. In another saucepan, melt the butter and whisk in 50 g / 2 oz of the flour; cook over a low heat, whisking constantly, for 4 minutes. Gradually add the milk, whisking all the time, and cook for 4–5 minutes.

Remove from the heat and beat in the grated cheeses; season well with salt, pepper and nutmeg. Pour the mixture into a 2.5 cm / 1 inch deep baking tin lined with clingfilm. Leave to cool for about 1 hour, then place in the refrigerator to set firm.

Put the breadcrumbs and the remaining flour on two plates. Beat the eggs in a mixing bowl. Remove the cheese mixture from the refrigerator and use the clingfilm to lift it out of the baking tin. Cut the cheese mixture into rectangular pieces, about 10 x 2.5 cm / 4 x 1 inch.

Dip each piece into the plate of flour, then into the beaten eggs and finally in the breadcrumbs to coat evenly. Place in the refrigerator for 30 minutes.

To serve, heat the oil for deep-frying. Deep-fry the parsley for 1 minute, until it is crisp, then drain on paper towels. Deep-fry the cheese croquettes for 3–4 minutes, until golden brown; drain on

CROQUETTES DE CREVETTES GRISES
(SHRIMP AND BRANDY BISQUE CROQUETTES)

SERVES 4

400 g / 14 oz unpeeled brown shrimps
3 gelatine leaves
50 g / 2 oz butter
150 g / 5 oz plain flour
1 tablespoon brandy
1 tablespoon tomato purée
salt and pepper
200 g / 7 oz peeled brown shrimps
150 g / 5 oz breadcrumbs
2 eggs
vegetable oil for deep-frying

Put the unpeeled shrimps in a saucepan filled with 500 ml / 16 fl oz water. Bring to the boil, then place the shrimps and water in a liquidizer and blend until smooth; rub through a sieve.

Soak the gelatine leaves in cold water until they are soft. Melt the butter in a saucepan and whisk in 50 g / 2 oz of the flour; cook over a low heat, whisking constantly, for 4 minutes. Gradually add the shrimp liquid, whisking all the time. Beat in the brandy, tomato purée and the softened gelatine; season well. Cook the mixture until it thickens, then stir in the peeled shrimps.

Pour the mixture into a 2.5 cm / 1 inch deep baking tin lined with clingfilm. Leave to cool for about 1 hour, then place in the refrigerator to set firm.

Put the breadcrumbs and the remaining flour on two plates. Beat the eggs in a mixing bowl. Remove the shrimp mixture from the refrigerator and use the clingfilm to lift it out of the baking tin. Cut the shrimp mixture into rectangular pieces, about 10 x 2.5 cm / 4 x 1 inch.

Dip each piece into the plate of flour, then into the beaten eggs and finally in the breadcrumbs to coat evenly. Place in the refrigerator for 30 minutes.

To serve, heat the oil for deep-frying. Deep-fry the parsley for 1 minute, until it is crisp, then drain on paper towels. Deep-fry the shrimp croquettes for 3–4 minutes, until golden brown; drain on paper towels. Serve hot, garnished with salad leaves and half a lemon.

Croquettes de poulet
(Chicken croquettes)

SERVES 4
2 chicken legs
1 carrot, halved
1 onion, halved
1 sprig of thyme
1 bayleaf
3 cloves
3 gelatine leaves
50 g / 2 oz butter
150 g / 5 oz plain flour
1 teaspoon chopped fresh tarragon
50 ml / 2 fl oz double cream
salt and pepper
150 g / 2 oz breadcrumbs
2 eggs
vegetable oil for deep-frying
bunch of curly parsley

Put the chicken in a saucepan with 1 litre / 1¾ pints water, the carrot, onion, thyme, bayleaf and cloves. Bring to the boil and simmer for 1 hour.

Remove the chicken and boil the cooking liquid to reduce it to 300 ml / ½ pint. Strain the stock. Meanwhile, cut the chicken meat into small pieces.

Soak the gelatine leaves in cold water until they are soft. Melt the butter in a saucepan and whisk in 50 g / 2 oz of the flour; cook over a low heat, whisking constantly, for 4 minutes. Gradually add the chicken stock, whisking all the time, and cook the mixture for 5–6 minutes.

Beat in the softened gelatine, chicken pieces, tarragon and cream; season well. Pour the mixture into a 2.5 cm / 1 inch deep baking tin lined with clingfilm. Leave to cool for about 1 hour, then place in the refrigerator to set firm.

Coat the chicken mixture in flour, eggs and breadcrumbs as for shrimp croquettes. Chill, deep-fry and serve in the same way.

Salade liegeoise
(Warm salad with bacon, new potatoes and green beans)

SERVES 4

16 new potatoes

400 g / 14 oz green beans

8 rashers of smoked bacon

1 onion, finely chopped

4 tomatoes, quartered

200 ml / 7 fl oz vinaigrette dressing

2 tablespoons chopped fresh parsley

300 g / 11 oz mixed salad leaves

Cook the potatoes and green beans in salted boiling water until just tender. Drain, and refresh the beans in cold running water. Cut the potatoes in half.

Meanwhile, cut the bacon into thin strips and place under a hot grill until crisp.

Reheat the potatoes and beans in boiling water, then mix them with the onion, tomatoes, three-quarters of the vinaigrette and the parsley. Place the mixture in a dome shape on four serving plates and scatter the crisp bacon over the top. Toss the salad leaves with the remaining vinaigrette and arrange around the serving plates.

Witloof au gratin
(Braised chicory with ham and cheese sauce)

SERVES 2

4 heads of chicory

2 tablespoons brown sugar

juice of 1 lemon

salt and pepper

freshly grated nutmeg

500 ml / 16 fl oz milk

1 bay leaf

10 peppercorns

1 sprig of thyme

1 slice of onion

50 g / 2 oz butter

50 g / 2 oz plain flour

4 slices of Ardennes ham

50 g / 2 oz grated Gruyère

50 g / 2 oz grated Cheddar

Preheat the oven to 180° C / 350° F / Gas Mark 4.

Cut the cores out of the chicory from the base, leaving them whole. Place on a small baking sheet and sprinkle with brown sugar, lemon juice, salt, pepper, nutmeg and water to half cover them. Cover with foil and bake for 20 minutes. Remove the foil and bake for a further 20 minutes. Turn the chicory and bake for a further 20 minutes. Drain well.

Put the milk in a saucepan with the bay leaf, peppercorns, thyme and onion, bring to the boil, then set aside.

In another saucepan, melt the butter and whisk in the flour. Cook over a low heat, whisking constantly, for 1–2 minutes. Gradually pour in the milk through a strainer, whisking all the time. Bring the sauce back to the boil and cook for 3–4 minutes, whisking constantly until it thickens. Season to taste with salt, pepper and nutmeg.

Wrap a slice of ham around each head of chicory and place in two individual gratin dishes. Pour the sauce over, sprinkle with the cheese and heat through in the oven for 15–20 minutes, then place under a hot grill until the cheese is golden brown and bubbling. Serve hot.

Anguilles au vert
(Eels in green sauce)

SERVES 4
12 new potatoes
750 ml / 1¼ pints fish stock
200 ml / 7 fl oz wheat beer
800 g / 1¾ lb eels
2 bunches of watercress
1 tablespoon chopped fresh dill
1 tablespoon chopped fresh chives
200 ml / 7 fl oz double cream
salt and pepper

Cook the potatoes in salted boiling water until just tender.

Put the fish stock and beer in a wide saucepan and bring to a simmer.

Cut the eels into 5 cm / 2 inch pieces, then poach them in the stock for 4–5 minutes. Drain and set aside.

Chop the watercress leaves with the dill and chives as finely as possible, or purée in a liquidizer.

Boil the fish stock to reduce by two-thirds, then add the cream and the watercress purée. Whisk together and season well. Add the eels and potatoes and reheat gently for 3–4 minutes. Serve in soup plates.

Cabillaud à la flamande
(Flemish-style cod)

SERVES 4
20 new potatoes
4 hard-boiled eggs
4 cod steaks, about 175 g / 6 oz each
salt and pepper
85 g / 3 oz plain flour
125 g / 4 oz butter
1 tablespoon chopped fresh parsley
juice of 2 lemons

Preheat the oven to 200° C / 400° F / Gas Mark 6.

Cook the potatoes in salted boiling water until just tender. Peel the hard-boiled eggs and chop finely.

Season the cod and toss in flour to coat. Heat the butter in a frying pan, add the cod and fry until lightly browned on both sides. Transfer the fish to a dish and place in the oven for about 2 minutes or until cooked through.

Place the frying pan over moderate heat, add the egg and heat through for 1 minute, then add the chopped parsley and lemon juice. Put the cod on four warmed serving plates and pour the egg mixture over it. Serve with the boiled potatoes.

Raie au beurre noir
(Skate with black butter)

SERVES 2
10 new potatoes
2 skate wings, about 275 g / 10 oz each
50 g / 2 oz plain flour, seasoned
100 g / 3½ oz butter
1 tablespoon capers, rinsed
juice of 1 lemon
1 tablespoon chopped fresh parsley

Preheat the oven to 200° C / 400° F / Gas Mark 6.

Cook the potatoes in salted boiling water until just tender.

Using scissors, trim the skate wings, removing the outside bones. Toss in the seasoned flour.

Heat the butter in a wide, ovenproof frying pan until golden brown. Add the skate wings and cook for 2 minutes on each side or until well coloured. Put the pan in the oven for 4–5 minutes or until the fish is cooked through.

Place the fish on two warmed serving plates. Put the pan over a moderate heat, add the capers and cook, stirring, for 30 seconds. Add the lemon juice and chopped parsley and pour it over the skate. Serve at once, with the boiled potatoes.

Sole à l'oostendaise
(Sole with mussels and shrimps)

SERVES 4
400 ml / 14 fl oz fish stock
200 ml / 7 fl oz double cream
beurre manié (1 tablespoon butter mashed with 1 tablespoon
    flour until smooth)
200 ml / 7 fl oz wheat beer
2 globe artichokes
1 lemon, halved
12 new potatoes
4 lemon sole fillets, about 175 g / 6 oz each
8-12 mussels, freshly cooked
85 g / 3 oz peeled brown shrimps

COURT BOUILLON
125 ml / 4 fl oz dry white wine
1 carrot, and 1 small onion, sliced
1 sprig of thyme, 1 bay leaf, 3 cloves

For the court bouillon, put all the ingredients in a saucepan with 500 ml / 16 fl oz water, cover and simmer for 20 minutes.

Put the fish stock in a saucepan and boil to reduce by half. Add the cream and boil for 1 minute, then whisk in the beurre manié to thicken the sauce. Whisk in the beer.

Snap off the artichoke stems, cut off all the leaves and rub the artichoke bottoms with the lemon. Bring a saucepan of water to the boil, add the lemon halves and artichoke bottoms and cook for 15–20 minutes, until tender. Refresh under cold running water. Scoop out the chokes with a teaspoon. Boil the potatoes until just tender, then drain and set aside with the artichoke bottoms.

Roll up the fish fillets and hold in place with a cocktail stick. Poach the fish in the court bouillon for 3–4 minutes, until just cooked, then drain.

Reheat the beer cream sauce, adding the mussels, shrimps, potatoes and quartered artichoke bottoms. Remove the cocktail sticks from the fish and arrange on four warmed plates. Arrange the remaining ingredients on the plates and pour the sauce over.

Lotte aux poireaux
(Monkfish with leeks)

SERVES 4
600 g / 1¼ lb leeks
12 new potatoes
600 ml / 1 pint fish stock
200 ml / 7 fl oz wheat beer
675 g / 1½ lb monkfish fillet
200 ml / 7 fl oz double cream
salt and pepper

Clean the leeks thoroughly and slice them finely. Cook in a saucepan of boiling water for 2 minutes, then drain and refresh under cold running water. Cook the potatoes until just tender, then drain, refresh under cold water and set aside with the leeks.

Put the fish stock in a saucepan with the beer and boil to reduce the liquid by half.

Cut the monkfish into 1 cm / ½ inch slices and poach in the reduced stock for 2 minutes.

Add the cream, potatoes, leeks and seasoning and simmer gently for 4–5 minutes. Serve in soup plates.

Poussin à l'estragon
(Tarragon spring chicken)

SERVES 2
2 poussins
salt and pepper
freshly grated nutmeg
2 tablespoons vegetable oil
50 g / 2 oz butter
2 sprigs of thyme
150 ml / ¼ pint chicken stock
1 tablespoon chopped fresh tarragon
100 ml / 3½ fl oz double cream

Preheat the oven to 200° C / 400° F / Gas Mark 6.

Season the poussins inside and out with salt, pepper and nutmeg. Heat the oil and butter in a large frying pan, add the poussins and brown on all sides.

Transfer to a flameproof casserole and add the thyme. Place in the oven for 20–30 minutes or until cooked.

Remove from the oven, add the chicken stock and tarragon to the casserole and simmer over medium-high heat until the liquid is slightly reduced. Add the cream and bring back to the boil, then serve at once. Roast potatoes are the ideal accompaniment.

Poussin à la brabançonne
(Spring chicken with genever sauce and caramelized chicory)

SERVES 2

4 heads of chicory
85 g / 3 oz brown sugar
salt and pepper
freshly grated nutmeg
100 g / 3½ oz butter
2 poussins
2 tablespoons vegetable oil
1 measures (25 ml / 1 fl oz) clear genever
100 ml / 3½ fl oz chicken stock

Preheat the oven to 180° C / 350° F / Gas Mark 4.

Cut the cores out of the chicory from the base, leaving them whole. Place on a small baking sheet and sprinkle with brown sugar, salt, pepper, nutmeg, half the butter and about 4 tablespoons water. Place in the oven for 45 minutes, turning them halfway through the cooking time.

Season the poussins inside and out. Heat the remaining butter with the oil in a roasting tin, add the poussins and brown on all sides. Place in the oven for 20–30 minutes or until cooked.

Remove from the oven, add the clear genever and the chicken stock and boil for 1 minute.

Place the caramelized chicory on warmed plates with the poussins on top. Pour the sauce around them and serve with stoemp (see page 108).

Filet american
(Steak tartare)

SERVES 1

175 g / 6 oz beef fillet

40 g / 1½ oz gherkins, finely chopped

40 g / 1½ oz shallots, finely chopped

40 g / 1½ oz capers, chopped

2 drops of Tabasco sauce

2 tablespoons mayonnaise

salt and pepper

Finely mince the beef and mix with the chopped gherkins, shallots and capers. Stir in the Tabasco, mayonnaise and salt and pepper to taste.

Mould the mixture to resemble the shape of a fillet steak and place on a serving plate. Garnish with salad leaves and two or three gherkins and small pickled onions. Ideally, serve with frites.

WATERZOOI

Waterzooi aux poissons
(Mixed fish in a cream sauce)

Waterzooi is as Belgian as Tintin. This is a dish that dates back a few hundred years. Waterzooi simply means boiled or stewed in water. It was originally made using freshwater fish and rough cuts of vegetables, which were cooked together in water with thyme and bay leaves. Fresh cream would be added just before serving. The freshwater fish version was later replaced by waterzooi à la gantoise, which uses chicken instead of fish and lemon and black pepper to flavour.

In fact, this cooking concept permits you to use what you want. At Belgo we also cook our own version of the waterzooi: aux poissons de la Mer du Nord. This recipe is made with a combination of salmon, red and grey mullet and crayfish.

SERVES 4
300 g / 11 oz carrots
300 g / 11 oz celeriac
300 g / 11 oz trimmed leeks
600 ml / 1 pint fish stock
200 ml / 7 fl oz wheat beer
200 ml / 7 fl oz double cream
12 new potatoes
4 pieces of salmon fillet, about 85 g / 3 oz each
4 red mullet fillets, about 85 g / 3 oz each
4 pieces of grey mullet fillet, about 85 g / 3 oz each
2 teaspoons tomato purée
8–12 mussels, well scrubbed
12 crayfish (preferably live)
salt and pepper
chopped fresh parsley

Peel the carrots and celeriac. Cut all the vegetables into very fine (julienne) strips and cook in separate saucepans of salted boiling water for 2–3 minutes. Drain and refresh under cold running water.

Put the fish stock and beer in a saucepan and boil to reduce by half. Add the cream. Reduce the heat to a simmer, add the potatoes and cook for 10–15 minutes, until nearly tender.

Add the fish and simmer for a further 5 minutes. Add the tomato purée and mussels and boil for 2 minutes. Add the crayfish and vegetables and cook for 2–3 minutes. Season with salt and pepper and serve in soup plates, sprinkled with chopped parsley.

Waterzooi de lotte
(Monkfish in a cream sauce)

SERVES 4
300 g / 11 oz carrots
300 g / 11 oz celeriac
300 g / 11 oz trimmed leeks
12 new potatoes
750 ml / 1¼ pints fish stock
125 ml / 4 fl oz wheat beer
12 crayfish (preferably live)
675 g / 1½ lb monkfish fillet, cut into chunks
200 ml / 7 fl oz double cream
salt and pepper

Peel the carrots and celeriac. Cut all the vegetables into very fine (julienne) strips and cook in separate saucepans of boiling salted water for 2–3 minutes. Drain and refresh under cold running water. Cook the potatoes until just tender and set aside with the vegetables.

Put the fish stock and beer in a saucepan, bring to the boil and add the live crayfish, if using. After 2–3 minutes, remove the crayfish and set aside.

Boil the stock until it is reduced by half. Reduce the heat, add the monkfish and poach for 2 minutes. Add the cream and season to taste. Add the crayfish, vegetables and potatoes and heat through for 2–3 minutes. Serve in soup plates.

Waterzooi à la gantoise
(Chicken in a vegetable, cream and lemon sauce)

SERVES 4
300 g / 11 oz celeriac
300 g / 11 oz carrots
300 g / 11 oz trimmed leeks
12 new potatoes
600 ml / 1 pint chicken stock
200 ml / 7 fl oz lemon juice
salt and pepper
200 ml / 7 fl oz double cream
4 large chicken breasts
chopped fresh parsley

Peel the celeriac and carrots. Cut all the vegetables into very fine (julienne) strips and cook in separate saucepans of salted boiling water until they are just tender, but still slightly crisp to the bite. Drain and refresh under cold running water. Cook the potatoes until just tender and set aside with the vegetables.

Put the chicken stock in a saucepan with the lemon juice, salt and quite a lot of pepper to 'lift' the sauce. Bring to the boil, then add the cream. Cut each chicken breast into three equal pieces and add to the creamy chicken stock. Simmer gently for 8–10 minutes or until cooked through.

Add the cooked potatoes and vegetable strips and cook for a further 2–3 minutes. Serve in soup plates, sprinkled with chopped parsley.

Waterzooi de homard
(Lobster and Mussels with Vegetables)

SERVES 2

150 g / 5 oz carrots

150 g / 5 oz celeriac

150 g / 5 oz trimmed leeks

6 new potatoes

1 whole lobster (about 500 g / 1 lb 2 oz), cooked

200 ml / 7 fl oz Lobster bisque (see page 31)

10 mussels, well scrubbed

chopped fresh parsley

Peel the carrots and celeriac. Cut all the vegetables into very fine (julienne) strips and cook in separate saucepans of salted boiling water until they are just tender, but still slightly crisp to the bite. Drain and refresh under cold running water. Cook the potatoes until just tender and set aside with the vegetables.

Cut the lobster lengthways and then in half, separating the body and claws from the tail.

Put the lobster bisque in a wide saucepan to heat through. Add the lobster and mussels and simmer for 5 minutes. Add the potatoes and vegetables and simmer for a further 2 minutes.

To serve, divide the lobster and mussels between two soup plates, pour the sauce over the top and sprinkle with chopped parsley.

Bloedpans au vinaigre de xérès (Black pudding with sherry vinegar)

SERVES 2
2 apples
75 g / 3 oz brown sugar
125 g / 4 oz butter
300 g / 11 oz black pudding
2 tablespoons sherry vinegar
salt and pepper

Peel and halve the apples and take out the cores. Cut each half into three pieces and toss in the brown sugar. Melt 75 g / 3 oz of the butter in a frying pan, add the apple pieces and cook over a low heat until they are tender and brown. Remove from the pan and keep warm.

Cut the black pudding into 12 slices and fry in the same pan for 4 minutes. Arrange the apple slices in a fan or ring shape on two warmed plates. Remove the black pudding from the pan and place on the plates with the apple.

Add the sherry vinegar to the frying pan stir and cook, stirring, for 1 minute. Whisk the remaining butter into the pan to complete the sauce. Season to taste, then pour the sauce over the apples and black pudding and serve hot.

Stoemp saucisse (Belgian sausages and mash)

SERVES 4
4–6 potatoes
50 g / 2 oz butter
1 carrot, diced
1 leek, chopped
¼ head of Savoy cabbage, shredded
12 good pork or wild boar sausages
150 ml / ¼ pint double cream
salt and pepper
freshly grated nutmeg

Boil the potatoes until tender, drain and mash.

Melt half the butter in a saucepan, add the carrot, cover and cook over a very low heat for 5–10 minutes. Add the leek and cabbage and continue to cook until all the vegetables are tender.

Meanwhile, grill or fry the sausages until cooked through.

To serve, reheat the mashed potato. Beat in the remaining butter and the cream. Season to taste with salt, pepper and nutmeg and stir in the vegetables. Serve hot, surrounded by the sausages.

Pâte sucrée
(Sweet pastry case)

MAKES A 25 cm / 10 inch PASTRY CASE
200 g / 7 oz plain flour
85 g / 3½ oz caster sugar
100 g / 3½ oz butter, softened
1 egg yolk

Preheat the oven to 180° C / 350° F / Gas Mark 4.

Sift the flour into a bowl and stir in the sugar. Add the butter and egg yolk and mix lightly with your fingertips until the mixture forms coarse crumbs. Add about 1 tablespoon ice-cold water and mix lightly to form a dough. Wrap the dough and leave to rest in the refrigerator for 20-30 minutes.

Roll out the pastry to about 5 mm / ¼ inch thick and use to line a 25 cm / 10 inch tart tin. Cover the pastry with foil and fill with baking beans. Place in the hot oven for 10 minutes, then remove the foil and beans and cook for a further 5 minutes. Remove from the oven and leave to cool slightly.

Tarte au citron
(Lemon tart)

SERVES 6
150 ml / ¼ pint lemon juice
grated zest of 3 lemons
300 g / 11 oz caster sugar
7 eggs
250 ml / 8 fl oz double cream
1 cooked pastry case (see above)

Preheat the oven to 120° C / 250° F / Gas Mark ½.

Mix together the lemon juice and zest, sugar, eggs and cream. Pour the mixture into the pastry case and bake for about 15–20 minutes or until firm. Leave to cool, then chill in the refrigerator until ready to serve.

Tarte au sucre
(Almond cream tart)

SERVES 4–6
250 g / 9 oz caster sugar
50 g / 2 oz ground almonds
1 cooked pastry case (see left)
3 eggs
200 ml / 7 fl oz crème fraîche
½ teaspoon vanilla essence
50 g / 2 oz butter
50 g / 2 oz icing sugar

Preheat the oven to 180° C / 350° F / Gas Mark 4.

Mix the caster sugar with the ground almonds and spread evenly in the pastry case.

Beat together the eggs, crème fraîche and vanilla essence and pour into the pastry case. Cover with tiny knobs of butter and bake for about 30 minutes or until the filling is firm. Leave to cool. To serve, sift the icing sugar over the tart.

Tarte au riz
(Creamy rice tart)

SERVES 4–6
200 g / 7 oz pudding rice
250 ml / 8 fl oz double cream
750 ml / 1¼ pints milk
85 g / 3 oz caster sugar
½ teaspoon vanilla essence
1 cooked pastry case (see above)

Put the rice, cream, milk, caster sugar and vanilla essence in a saucepan and simmer gently for about 1 hour, stirring frequently.

Preheat the oven to 180° C / 350° F / Gas Mark 4.

When the rice has absorbed all the liquid, pour into the pastry case and bake for 10 minutes. Leave to cool before serving.

BELGO'S TOP 10 FILMS TO WATCH

1. **THE SEXUAL LIFE OF THE BELGIANS**
2. **TOTO LE HERO**
3. **DAËNS**
4. **MAN BITES DOG** (*after dinner only*)
5. **TINTIN SUR LA LUNE**
6. **IF IT'S TUESDAY THIS MUST BE BELGIUM**
7. **BABETTE'S FEAST**
8. **LA GRANDE BOUFFE**
9. **UN HOMME ET UNE FEMME**
10. **WITHNAIL AND I**

Mousse au chocolat belge
(Belgian chocolate mousse)

SERVES 4
150 g / 5 oz chocolate (dark, milk or white)
2 eggs, separated
25 g / 1 oz caster sugar
300 ml / ½ pint whipping cream

Cut the chocolate into small pieces and place in a bowl over a small saucepan of very hot water. Stir until melted and smooth, then leave to cool.

Mix the egg yolks with half the sugar. Whip the cream until it starts to thicken, but is not stiff.

Whip the egg whites with the remaining sugar until stiff, then gently fold into the cream. Gradually add the egg yolk and sugar mixture, then finally fold in the melted chocolate. Spoon into ramekins and leave to set for 4 hours before serving.

Café liegeois
(Coffee ice cream with whipped cream)

SERVES 1
100 ml / 3½ fl oz whipping cream
25 g / 1 oz icing sugar
1 tablespoon Camp coffee
100 ml / 3½ fl oz milk
3 scoops of mocha ice cream

Whip the cream until it starts to thicken, then add the icing sugar and whip until firm.

Mix half the coffee with the milk. Put the ice cream in a glass or bowl, add the coffee / milk mixture and top with the whipped cream. Pour the remaining Camp coffee over the top and serve at once.

Belgo specialities

ONCE WE FELT SATISFIED that Belgo had successfully introduced the wonderful simplicity of Belgian traditional cooking, we could not help being compelled to create our own signature dishes. We did this by using traditional methods or ingredients and giving them something of a modern twist.

Being in Britain gave us an opportunity to do this without having to worry too much about a Belgian public outcry for not using the beef drippings or tonnes of butter that some of the original recipes required. What we set out to do was to introduce a series of new dishes that would pay tribute to the ingredients and methods of the classic Belgian repertoire.

INSPECT A POIREAUX

ASPARAGUS

Asperges
(Asparagus)

We are often asked, "What will Belgo do if one day all the mussels in the world vanish?" Denis and André's response: "Let them eat asparagus!" So you think we lost our heads? We did that a long time ago. Quite seriously, most restaurants in Belgium, and also in the Netherlands and Germany, that have mainly mussels on their menu throughout the year usually replace them with a selection of asparagus when seasonal supplies of mussels diminish. It just so happens that the asparagus season in northern Europe starts as the mussels enter their spawning period.

Delicious white asparagus from Malines (Mechelen) in northern Belgium is renowned for its superb texture and juiciness. Green asparagus, from other parts of Belgium and from the Netherlands, is more readily available and not so expensive as the white "Malines".

Asparagus was introduced to Belgium during the period of Spanish rule and soon became a leading member of the Belgian culinary repertoire. We at Belgo make a point of celebrating asparagus all year round by giving it its own section on our menu.

SERVES 1
8 asparagus spears
salt

Trim the base of the asparagus and peel about halfway up the stalks.

Place in a wide pan of boiling salted water and boil until just tender; 5–10 minutes, depending on size. Refresh under cold running water to set the green colour. Pat dry and chill until needed.

LET THEM EAT ASPARAGUS!

Asperges flamande
(Warm asparagus with butter and chopped eggs)

SERVES 2
16 cooked asparagus spears
125 g / 4 oz butter
1 hard-boiled egg, finely chopped
salt and pepper
juice of ½ lemon
1 teaspoon chopped fresh parsley

Place the asparagus in a pan of boiling water to heat through for 1–2 minutes. Drain, pat dry and arrange on two warmed serving plates.

Heat the butter in a frying pan until it is light brown, add the chopped egg and seasoning. Cook for 45 seconds, then add the lemon juice and pour over the warm asparagus. Sprinkle with parsley and serve at once.

Asperges meunière
(Warm asparagus with butter, lemon juice and parsley)

SERVES 1
8 cooked asparagus spears
50 g / 2 oz butter
juice of ½ lemon
1 teaspoon chopped fresh parsley
salt and pepper

Place the asparagus in a pan of boiling water to heat through for 1–2 minutes. Drain, pat dry and arrange on a warmed serving plate. Brown the butter in a frying pan and add the lemon juice, parsley and seasoning. Pour over the warm asparagus and serve at once.

117

Asperges hollandaise
(Warm asparagus with hollandaise sauce)

SERVES 2
125 g / 4 oz butter
2 egg yolks
2 tablespoons white wine
juice of ½ lemon
salt and pepper
16 cooked asparagus spears

First, clarify the butter by heating slowly in a saucepan and cooking gently for a few minutes. Leave to cool until tepid. Using a spoon, carefully skim the impurities off the top of the butter and pour the clarified butter into a small ramekin, taking care to leave behind the impurities at the bottom of the pan.

To make the hollandaise, first heat a saucepan of water. Place the egg yolks and wine in a round-bottomed bowl, mix well, then place the bowl over the saucepan of hot water and whisk until the mixture thickens; this will take about 3 minutes.

Remove the bowl from the heat and very gradually whisk in the clarified butter. Finally add the lemon juice and seasoning.

Place the asparagus in a pan of boiling water to heat through for 1–2 minutes. Drain, pat dry and arrange on two warmed serving plates. Pour the hollandaise over and serve at once.

Asperges vinaigrette
(Chilled asparagus with vinaigrette dressing)

SERVES 4
½ teaspoon Dijon mustard
½ teaspoon finely chopped shallots
½ teaspoon finely chopped garlic
½ teaspoon chopped fresh thyme
50 ml / 2 fl oz red wine vinegar
salt and pepper
200 ml / 7 fl oz vegetable oil
50 ml / 2 fl oz olive oil
32 cooked, chilled asparagus spears

Put the mustard, shallots, garlic, thyme, vinegar and seasoning in a bowl and whisk well. Mix the two oils together and incorporate them slowly into the mixture, whisking all the time.

Divide the asparagus spears between four serving plates and either pour the vinaigrette over them or serve it separately.

Asperges ardennaise
(Chilled asparagus with Ardennes ham)

SERVES 4

½ teaspoon Dijon mustard

½ teaspoon finely chopped shallots

½ teaspoon finely chopped garlic

½ teaspoon chopped fresh thyme

50 ml / 2 fl oz red wine vinegar

salt and pepper

200 ml / 7 fl oz vegetable oil

50 ml / 2 fl oz olive oil

32 cooked, chilled asparagus spears

8 slices of Ardennes ham

Put the mustard, shallots, garlic, thyme, vinegar and seasoning in a bowl and whisk well. Mix the two oils together and incorporate them slowly into the mixture, whisking all the time.

Divide the asparagus spears between four serving plates and either pour the vinaigrette over them or serve it separately.

Arrange 2 slices of Ardennes ham on each plate.

Asperges crevettes grises
(Chilled asparagus with brown shrimps)

SERVES 4

½ teaspoon Dijon mustard

½ teaspoon finely chopped shallots

½ teaspoon finely chopped garlic

½ teaspoon chopped fresh thyme

50 ml / 2 fl oz red wine vinegar

salt and pepper

200 ml / 7 fl oz vegetable oil

50 ml / 2 fl oz olive oil

32 cooked, chilled asparagus spears

325 g / 12 oz peeled brown shrimps

4 teaspoons chopped fresh chives

Put the mustard, shallots, garlic, thyme, vinegar and seasoning in a bowl and whisk well. Mix the two oils together and incorporate them slowly into the mixture, whisking all the time.

Put the asparagus on the serving plates. Mix the shrimps with the chives and scatter the shrimps over the top and pour on the vinaigrette.

LEEKS

POIREAUX
(LEEKS)

Leeks are tremendously versatile, delicious and cheap. They are also a great alternative to the more expensive and seasonal asparagus. They are hugely popular in Belgium and are used throughout the cooking repertoire, braised in butter, steamed or grilled. Leeks are just as popular in other northern European countries such as the Netherlands and Germany.

For those of you who may not know this, the French word for leeks is *poireaux*.

So when we introduced leeks to the Belgo menu we could hardly resist using our poor sense of humour and naming the section Poirot's poireaux!

SERVES 1
400 g / 14 oz leeks
1 teaspoon salt
juice of ½ lemon
salt and pepper

Bring a saucepan of water to the boil. Peel off the outer leaves of the leeks and trim the root end and the top green parts, so they are all of equal length. Wash them thoroughly.

Add the salt to the boiling water, then add the leeks and boil until they are tender right through when tested with the point of a sharp knife; this will take approximately 20 minutes, depending on size.

Mix the lemon juice with the salt and pepper and set aside. Refresh the leeks under cold running water, then gently squeeze them dry.

Place in a shallow dish, pour over the lemon juice and chill in the refrigerator.

They are now ready for the following recipes.

POIREAUX VINAIGRETTE
(Leeks with vinaigrette dressing)

¼ teaspoon Dijon mustard

½ garlic clove, finely chopped

½ teaspoon finely chopped shallot

good pinch of fresh thyme leaves, chopped

1 tablespoon red wine vinegar

salt and pepper

3 tablespoons sunflower oil

1 tablespoon olive oil

400 g / 14 oz cooked, chilled leeks

To make the vinaigrette, mix the mustard, garlic, shallot, thyme, vinegar and seasoning together in a small bowl. Whisk in the oils.

Simply pour the vinaigrette over the leeks and serve.

POIREAUX ARDENNAISE
(Leeks with Ardennes ham)

Follow the recipe for poireaux vinaigrette and arrange 2 slices of Ardennes ham on top.

POIREAUX CREVETTES GRISES
(Leeks with brown shrimps)

Follow the recipe for poireaux vinaigrette. Mix 75 g / 3 oz peeled brown shrimps with 1 teaspoon chopped fresh chives and scatter over the leeks.

LOBSTER

Homard à l'espagnole
(Lobster with garlic and olive oil)

On one of our early visits back to Belgium, while we were setting up Belgo, we met an old friend whose child was playing with the most unusual toy. It was the bottom half of a remote-controlled miniature sports car wearing the carcass of a freshly eaten lobster. He proceeded to race this "lobster" wherever we went: supermarkets, warehouse stores etc. He introduced his "pet" as "Homard Sharif" (*homard* being French for lobster). Quite what that little story has to do with explaining the popularity of lobsters in Belgium and on the Belgo menu we cannot answer, but we felt obliged to write it.

One thing that is for sure, though, is that lobster, *homard* in French or *kreeft* in Flemish, has an important place in the Belgian appetite. On the Place Sainte Catherine, where most of Brussels' seafood brokers and wholesalers are located, you will find five or six restaurants dedicating their menus entirely to the worship of this crustacean. Au Rugbyman restaurant celebrates the lobster in over 20 recipes. At Belgo we sell some 200 lobsters a week, served in four or five different ways. Here is one of the simplest. Salut Homard!

SERVES 1–2
1 lobster (about 500 g / 1 lb 2 oz)
2 garlic cloves
100 ml / 3½ fl oz extra virgin olive oil
chopped fresh parsley
1 lemon, halved

Preheat the grill. Using a heavy cleaver, chop the lobster in half lengthways. Peel the garlic and crush under the blade of the cleaver. Mix the garlic and olive oil together, then pour over the lobster. Place the lobster under the hot grill for about 8–10 minutes, until the flesh is just cooked and hot through. Sprinkle with parsley and serve at once, with half a lemon and salad leaves.

Omar who?

Soupe de moules
(Mussel, cream and saffron soup)

SERVES 4

1 kg / 2½ lb mussels, cleaned (see page 21)

1 litre / 1¾ pints dry white wine

50 g / 2 oz butter

1 onion, chopped

2 sticks of celery, chopped

4 leeks, chopped

generous pinch of saffron strands,
    infused in 2 tablespoons boiling water

250 ml / 8 fl oz double cream

beurre manié (1 tablespoon softened butter mashed with
    1 tablepoon plain flour until smooth)

julienne of vegetables (2 carrots and 1 leek, cut into very fine
    strips, blanched in boiling water and refreshed in cold water)

Put the mussels in a casserole with the wine, place over high heat and bring to the boil. Cook until the mussels have opened, stirring frequently to ensure they are evenly cooked; this takes only a few minutes.

Strain the cooking liquid through a fine sieve into a jug, leaving behind any grit. Add water to make up to 1 litre / 1¾ pints.

Discard any mussels that have not opened and remove the rest from their shells, discarding the shells.

Melt the butter in a large saucepan, add the chopped vegetables and cook over a low heat for 5 minutes, until softened but not browned. Reserve 20–30 mussels and add the rest to the vegetables, together with the strained cooking liquid; simmer for about 1 hour.

Blend the soup in a liquidizer and pass it through a conical sieve into the cleaned pan. Add the saffron and cream and reheat, whisking in the beurre manié to thicken the soup. Serve hot in soup plates, with the julienne of vegetables and 5–6 of the reserved mussels in each plate.

Mariage de moules et langoustines, sauce snob
(Mussels and langoustines in lobster sauce)

SERVES 2
1 kg / 2¼ lb mussels, cleaned
125 ml / 4 fl oz dry white wine
600 ml / 1 pint Lobster bisque (see page 31)
12 langoustines, cooked
1 tablespoon chopped fresh parsley

Put the mussels in a casserole with the wine, place over high heat and bring to the boil. Cook for a few minutes only, until the mussels have opened, stirring frequently to ensure they are evenly cooked. Discard any mussels that have not opened and remove the rest from their shells, discarding the shells.

Heat the lobster bisque in a pan, then add the mussels and langoustines and heat through.

Using a slotted spoon, put the mussels in the centre of two large soup plates and arrange the langoustines around the sides. Pour the sauce over the mussels and sprinkle with parsley. Serve at once.

Feuilleté de moules safrané
(Mussels and samphire in puff pastry)

SERVES 4
200 g / 7 oz puff pastry
200 ml / 7 fl oz double cream
1 teaspoon chopped shallots
generous pinch of saffron strands
400 g / 14 oz cooked, shelled mussels (see left)
salt and pepper
400 g / 14 oz fresh samphire

Preheat the oven to 220° C / 425° F / Gas Mark 7.

Roll out the puff pastry to about 5 mm / just under ¼ inch thick and cut out four squares. Place on a dampened baking sheet and bake for 8–10 minutes or until deep golden brown. Transfer to a wire rack and leave to cool.

Put the cream, shallots and saffron in a saucepan, add the mussels and a touch of seasoning and heat gently.

Cook the samphire in boiling water for 2 minutes. Drain well.

Slice the pastry squares through the middle and put the bases on four serving plates. Pour the mussels and their sauce over the pastry bases and put the samphire on top. Half-cover with the pastry tops and serve at once.

Escargots Ixelles
(Snail and mushroom tartlets)

SERVES 4
200 g / 7 oz puff pastry
4–6 heads of chicory
peanut / groundnut oil for deep-frying
50 g / 2 oz butter
2 cloves garlic, crushed
24 snails
100 g / 3½ oz mixed mushrooms, sliced
100 ml / 3½ fl oz dry white wine
1 tablespoon sherry vinegar

Preheat the oven to 220° C / 425° F / Gas Mark 7.

Roll out the puff pastry to about 5mm / just under ¼ inch thick and cut out four squares. Place on a dampened baking sheet and bake for 8–10 minutes or until deep golden brown. Transfer to a wire rack and leave to cool.

Cut the chicory in half lengthways and cut out the cores. Slice the chicory very thinly. Heat the oil for deep-frying, add the chicory and fry for 1 minute. Remove from the pan and drain for 5 minutes.

Just before serving, reheat the oil and deep-fry the chicory again until it is well browned.

Melt the butter in a frying pan and add the garlic, snails and mushrooms. Sauté for 5 minutes, then add the wine and vinegar and cook for 2 minutes.

Slice the pastry squares through the middle and put the bases on four serving plates. Spoon the snail mixture over the pastry bases and put the deep-fried chicory on top. Half-cover with the pastry tops and serve at once.

Salade de Herve piquante
(Belgian cheese salad)

SERVES 2
4 Little Gem lettuce
2 tablespoons finely chopped chives
3 tablespoons olive oil
1 tablespoon lemon juice
2 Golden Delicious apples
200 g / 7 oz Herve piquante cheese

Rinse the lettuce and shred about half of it, reserving 20–25 attractive leaves. Put the chives in a bowl with the olive oil and lemon juice and mix well.

Peel and core the apples and cut into dice. Cut the cheese into similar-sized dice.

Mix the shredded lettuce with half the chive dressing. Place the reserved leaves upright around the sides of two individual salad bowls and put the shredded leaves in the centre.

Toss the apples and cheese with the remaining dressing and spoon the mixture over the shredded lettuce.

Salade de pigeon
(Warm pigeon salad)

SERVES 2

2 slices of bread, crusts removed, cubed

25 g / 1 oz pine kernels

2 pigeon breasts

50 g / 2 oz butter

85 g / 3 oz smoked bacon, thinly sliced

100 g / 3½ oz mushrooms, thinly sliced

2 tablespoons sherry vinegar

2 large handfuls of mixed lettuce leaves

VINAIGRETTE

¼ teaspoon Dijon mustard

½ garlic clove, finely chopped

½ teaspoon finely chopped shallot

good pinch of fresh thyme leaves, chopped

1 tablespoon red wine vinegar

salt and pepper

3 tablespoons sunflower oil

1 tablespoon olive oil

Preheat the oven to 200° C / 400° F / Gas Mark 6. Heat the grill and grill the bread cubes until evenly browned. Grill the pine kernels until lightly browned – do not let them burn. Set aside.

To make the vinaigrette, place all the ingredients in a screw-topped jar and shake well.

Season the pigeon breasts. Melt the butter in an ovenproof pan and add the pigeon, bacon and mushrooms. When the pigeon is browned on both sides, put the pan in the hot oven. After 2 minutes, remove the pigeon to a warmed dish. Leave the mushrooms and bacon in the oven until cooked through, then transfer them to the dish with the pigeon. Place the pan over moderate heat, add the vinegar and cook, stirring, for 1 minute.

Slice the pigeon. Toss the lettuce with a little vinaigrette and arrange in the centre of two plates. Scatter the mushrooms and bacon around the outside. Put the sliced pigeon on the lettuce. Sprinkle with the croûtons and pine kernels; serve at once.

Choucroute forestière
(Sauerkraut with mushrooms)

SERVES 2

500 g / 1 lb 2 oz sauerkraut

85 g / 3 oz butter

200 g / 7 oz flat mushrooms, sliced

200 g / 7 oz oyster mushrooms, sliced if large

100 ml / 3½ fl oz dry white wine

10 asparagus spears

150 ml / ¼ pint double cream

1 teaspoon Dijon mustard

Rinse and drain the sauerkraut. Melt the butter in a saucepan and add the mushrooms. Cook gently for 3–4 minutes, then add the sauerkraut and wine. Leave over a very low heat for 10 minutes, stirring occasionally.

Peel the asparagus and cook in salted boiling water until just tender. Drain well.

Put the cream and mustard in a small saucepan and heat gently – do not boil.

Put the sauerkraut and mushroom mixture in the centre of two warmed serving dishes. Pour the cream sauce around it and arrange the asparagus on the sauce. Serve at once.

Choucroute safranée
(Saffron sauerkraut with seafood)

SERVES 2

500 g / 1 lb 2 oz sauerkraut

pinch of saffron strands

1 sprig of thyme

100 ml / 3½ fl oz mussel or fish stock

100 ml / 3½ fl oz dry white wine

150 g / 5 oz red mullet

150 g / 5 oz grey mullet

150 g / 5 oz cod

8–10 mussels, cleaned

salt

4–6 new potatoes, boiled

Rinse and drain the sauerkraut. Put the saffron, thyme, mussel or fish stock and white wine in a saucepan and bring to a simmer. Reduce the heat and add the sauerkraut, fish and mussels. Place the lid on the pan and cook for 8–10 minutes or until the fish is cooked and the mussels have opened.

Taste the sauerkraut and season if necessary. Put the sauerkraut in the centre of two warmed serving plates. Pour on a little of the cooking juices, then arrange the fish and potatoes around the sides.

Saumon à la Hoegaarden
(Salmon with wheat beer sauce)

SERVES 4

400 ml / 14 fl oz fish stock

200 ml / 7 fl oz crème fraîche

beurre manié (1 tablespoon butter mashed
    with 1 tablespoon flour)

200 ml / 7 fl oz Hoegaarden white beer

25 g / 1 oz pistachio nuts, finely chopped

4 pieces of salmon fillet, about 200 g / 7 oz each

a little flour, for dusting the fish

oil and butter, for frying

CARAMELIZED CHICORY

4 heads of chicory

1 teaspoon sugar

generous pinch of nutmeg

salt and pepper

To make the caramelized chicory, cut the chicory into thin slices and place in a heavy-bottomed saucepan with the sugar, nutmeg, salt, pepper and 2 tablespoons water. Cook over a high heat, stirring frequently, until the chicory begins to brown, then gradually reduce the heat, stirring from time to time until the chicory is evenly browned and tender.

Meanwhile, boil the fish stock over a high heat to reduce the liquid by half. Add the cream and boil to reduce slightly, then whisk in the beurre manié to thicken the sauce, and add the beer and pistachio nuts. Lightly dust the salmon with flour, then fry the fillets in oil and butter. Divide the caramelized chicory between four warmed serving plates. Place the salmon on the chicory and pour the sauce around the fish. Serve with mangetout and boiled potatoes.

Sole à la zeebrugeoise
(Sole with lobster sauce)

SERVES 4

300 ml / 10 fl oz dry white wine

1 bouquet garni (celery, leek, thyme, black peppercorns,
  bayleaf, parsley)

1 carrot, sliced

1 small onion, sliced

4 Dover sole fillets, about 175 g / 6 oz each

20 mussels, cleaned

75 ml Lobster bisque (see page 31)

150 g / 5 oz peeled brown shrimps

3 new potatoes, boiled

Put the wine in a saucepan with the bouquet garni, carrot, onion
and 150 ml / ¼ pint water, bring to the boil and then reduce the
heat to a simmer. Roll up the sole fillets and hold in place with a
cocktail stick. Put them in the simmering liquid, add the mussels
and poach slowly for 6–8 minutes.

Meanwhile, heat the lobster bisque in a saucepan, then add
the shrimps and heat through gently.

Drain the sole fillets, remove the cocktail sticks and arrange
on four warmed plates. Pour the lobster sauce over the sole and
arrange the potatoes and mussels around the side. Serve at once.

Turbot, sauce nero
(Turbot with squid ink sauce)

SERVES 4

900 g / 2 lb spinach

2–3 sprigs of thyme

2 bayleaves

10 black peppercorns

2 shallots, sliced

4 turbot fillets, about 175 g / 6 oz each

200 ml / 7 fl oz double cream

beurre manié (1 tablespoon butter mashed with
  1 tablespoon flour)

200 ml / 7 fl oz Hoegaarden white beer

4–6 heads of chicory

peanut / groundnut oil for deep-frying

2 sachets (about 5 g / ¼ oz each) of squid ink

salt and pepper

100 g / 3½ oz butter

Cook the spinach in a saucepan of salted boiling water for 1
minute. Drain, refresh under cold running water, then squeeze out
all the moisture. Set aside.

Put the thyme, bayleaves, peppercorns and shallots into a
wide saucepan with 600 ml / 1 pint water. Bring slowly to the boil
and simmer for 15 minutes, then add the turbot and poach gently
for 5 minutes. Lift out the fish and set aside, covered, in a warm
place. Strain the liquid into a measuring jug.

Pour 400 ml / 14 fl oz of the liquid into a saucepan and boil
over a high heat to reduce the liquid by half. Add the cream and
boil to reduce slightly, then whisk in the beurre manié to thicken
the sauce, and add the beer. Set aside.

Cut the chicory in half lengthways and cut out the cores. Slice
the chicory very thinly. Heat the oil for deep-frying, add the chicory
and fry until it is golden and crisp. Drain on paper towels.

Reheat the fish cream sauce over a low heat and whisk in the
squid ink. Season to taste. Reheat the spinach in the butter. Put
the spinach in the centre of four warmed serving plates and put
the turbot fillets on top. Pour the sauce around the spinach.
Scatter the deep-fried chicory over the fish and serve at once.

Ragoût de champignons à la Trappiste
(Mushrooms stewed in Orval beer, in a pastry case with Orval cheese)

SERVES 4

85 g / 3 oz butter

2 onions, thinly sliced

300 g / 11 oz flat mushrooms, thickly sliced

300 g / 11 oz oyster mushrooms, sliced if large

200 ml / 7 fl oz Orval beer

300 ml / ½ pint double cream

salt and pepper

300 g / 11 oz puff pastry

8 slices of Orval cheese

Preheat the oven to 220° C / 425° F / Gas Mark 7.

Melt the butter in a large saucepan, then add the onions and cook over a low heat for 5 minutes or until softened but not browned. Add the mushrooms and cook slowly for another 5 minutes, then add the beer, cream and seasoning and leave to simmer for 20–25 minutes.

Roll out the puff pastry to about 5 mm / just under ¼ inch thick and cut out four large squares. Place on a dampened baking sheet and bake for 10 minutes or until deep golden brown. Transfer to a wire rack for a few minutes.

Slice the pastry squares through the middle and put the bases on four heatproof serving dishes. Divide the mushroom mixture between the pastry bases and place two slices of cheese on each. Place under a hot grill for 5 seconds. Replace the pastry tops and serve at once.

Pintade au deux choux
(Guinea fowl with red cabbage and sauerkraut)

SERVES 2
250 g / 9 oz red cabbage
500 ml / 16 fl oz red wine
250 ml / 8 fl oz red wine vinegar
50 g / 2 oz brown sugar
½ an apple, diced
salt and pepper
75 g / 3 oz butter
1 guinea fowl
1 carrot, diced
1 small onion, chopped
1 sprig of thyme
1 bay leaf
100 ml / 3½ fl oz chicken stock
250 g / 9 oz sauerkraut

The day before you want to serve the dish, cut the red cabbage into very thin strips and put it in a bowl together with half the red wine, the vinegar, brown sugar, diced apple and a little salt and pepper. Leave to marinate overnight.

The next day, put the red cabbage and its marinade into a saucepan and cook over a low heat for 2–3 hours.

Preheat the oven to 180° C / 350° F / Gas Mark 4. Melt 65 g / 2½ oz of the butter in a roasting tin, add the guinea fowl and brown on all sides. Add the carrot, onion, thyme and bayleaf and roast in the oven for 20–25 minutes or until cooked.

Remove the guinea fowl from the roasting tin and keep warm. Pour off the fat and place the pan over medium-high heat. Add the remaining red wine and the chicken stock and stir to deglaze the pan. Boil until the sauce reduces and thickens, and finally whisk in the remaining 15 g / ½ oz of butter. Season to taste.

Heat the sauerkraut. Cut the guinea fowl in half and serve on warmed plates with the red cabbage and sauerkraut. Pour some of the sauce over the guinea fowl.

Cailles à l'ardennaise
(Quail with mushrooms and ham)

SERVES 2
75 g / 3 oz butter
200 g / 7 oz oyster mushrooms, chopped
salt and pepper
4 quails (preferably boned)
2 slices of Ardennes ham
200 ml / 7 fl oz chicken stock
3 tablespoons double cream
1 tablespoon chopped fresh chives

Preheat the oven to 200° C / 400° F / Gas Mark 6.

Melt 50 g / 2 oz of the butter in a frying pan, add the oyster mushrooms and cook for 2–3 minutes. Season to taste and then stuff the quails with the mushrooms. Wrap the quails tightly with the Ardennes ham. Melt the remaining butter in the frying pan, add the quails and brown lightly on all sides. Place the quails in the hot oven for 8–10 minutes or until just cooked. Remove from the oven and keep warm.

Pour off any excess fat from the frying pan, add the chicken stock and boil to reduce by three-quarters. Whisk in the cream and bring back to the boil.

Serve the quails on warmed plates with the sauce poured over them. Sprinkle with chopped chives and serve hot.

Crêpes
(Pancakes)

MAKES 4–6 CREPES
1 egg
25 g / 1 oz caster sugar
25 g / 1 oz plain flour, sifted
pinch of salt
25 g / 1 oz butter, melted
½ teaspoon vanilla essence
100 ml / 3½ fl oz milk
25 g / 1 oz butter for frying

Mix together the egg, sugar, flour, salt, melted butter and vanilla essence. Gradually pour in the milk, whisking constantly. Leave the mixture to rest for 20 minutes.

Heat a knob of butter in a frying pan over medium-high heat. Pour in a ladleful of the pancake batter and quickly tilt the pan so the batter just covers the base of the pan; it must not be too thick. Let it cook for about 2 minutes, then flip it over and cook the other side for 1 minute.

Repeat with the remaining batter, stacking the cooked pancakes on a warmed plate.

Crêpe flamande
(Pancake with caramelized apples and prunes, vanilla ice cream and white chocolate sauce)

SERVES 1
1 apple
50 g / 2 oz butter
5–6 canned prunes, drained, stones removed
50 g / 2 oz caster sugar
50 g / 2 oz white chocolate
85 ml / 3 fl oz milk
1 pancake (see left)
2 scoops of real vanilla ice cream

Peel and core the apple and cut it into quarters. Melt the butter in a saucepan, add the apple pieces and cook gently for 2 minutes. Add the prunes and the sugar, cover the pan with a lid and cook for a further 5 minutes.

Break the chocolate into a small saucepan and add the milk. Heat gently, whisking constantly. When hot and thick, remove from the heat and set aside.

Put the pancake on a warmed serving plate. Put the ice cream, apples and prunes on the pancake and fold over. Pour the white chocolate sauce around the pancake and serve at once.

CRÊPE BELGO
(PANCAKE WITH VANILLA ICE CREAM, MIXED BERRIES AND WHITE CHOCOLATE SAUCE)

SERVES 1
50 g / 2 oz white chocolate
85 ml / 3 fl oz milk
1 pancake (see left)
2 scoops of real vanilla ice cream
50 g / 2 oz mixed berries (raspberries, strawberries,
    blueberries, blackcurrants)

Break the chocolate into a small saucepan and add the milk. Heat gently, whisking constantly. When hot and thick, remove from the heat and set aside.

Put the pancake on a warmed serving plate. Put the ice cream and berries on the pancake and fold over. Pour the white chocolate sauce around the pancake and serve at once.

GAUFRES BELGO
(BELGIAN WAFFLES)

SERVES 4
100 ml / 3½ fl oz milk
40 g / 1½ oz butter
1 vanilla pod
175 g / 6 oz plain flour
15 g / ½ oz yeast
2 eggs, separated
15 g / ½ oz caster sugar
50 ml / 2 fl oz white beer (e.g. Hoegaarden)
50 g / 2 oz preserving sugar
2 tablespoons icing sugar
white chocolate sauce and mixed berries
    (see Crêpe Belgo, left)

Put the milk, butter and vanilla pod in a saucepan and bring to the boil. Remove from the heat and whisk in the flour. Cook over a low heat, stirring constantly, for 3–5 minutes. Leave to cool, then remove the vanilla pod.

Mix the yeast with 3 tablespoons water until evenly blended. Stir into the cooled milk mixture and leave for 1 hour.

Beat the egg yolks into the yeast mixture. In a bowl, whisk the egg whites until firm, add the sugar and a pinch of salt and continue whisking until stiff. Fold into the yeast mixture and leave for a further 1 hour.

Stir the beer into the mixture. To cook the waffles, pour the mixture into a waffle iron (fill the iron about a quarter full) and sprinkle with preserving sugar. Cook until the waffle is risen and golden brown.

Serve at once, sprinkled with icing sugar and accompanied by warm white chocolate sauce and mixed berries.

Tarte aux pruneaux et amandes
(Prune and almond tart)

SERVES 4–6
8 eggs
250 g / 9 oz caster sugar
200 g / 7 oz plain flour, sifted
½ teaspoon vanilla essence
100 g / 3½ oz ground almonds
400 g / 14 oz canned prunes in syrup, drained, stones removed
50 g / 2 oz icing sugar

FOR THE PASTRY CASE
200 g / 7 oz plain flour
85 g / 3½ oz caster sugar
100 g / 3½ oz butter, softened
1 egg yolk

Preheat the oven to 180° C / 350° F / Gas Mark 4.

To make the pastry case, sift the flour into a bowl and stir in the sugar. Add the butter and egg and mix lightly with your fingertips until the mixture forms coarse crumbs. Add about 1 tablespoon ice-cold water and mix lightly to form a dough. Wrap the dough and leave to rest in the refrigerator for 20–30 minutes.

Roll out the pastry to about 5 mm / ¼ inch thick and use to line a 25 cm / 10 inch tart tin. Cover the pastry with foil and fill with baking beans. Place in the hot oven for 10 minutes, then remove the foil and beans and cook for a further 5 minutes. Remove from the oven and leave to cool slightly.

Mix the eggs and caster sugar together in a large bowl. Bring a saucepan of water to the boil, then reduce the heat a little and put the mixing bowl over the pan. Whisk the mixture until it is warm and thick, then remove the bowl from the saucepan and continue whisking until the mixture is cold. Gradually fold the flour, vanilla essence and ground almonds into the mixture.

Put the prunes in the pastry case. Pour the egg mixture evenly over the prunes and bake for 10–15 minutes, or until the mixture is just firm to the touch. Dust with icing sugar before serving, warm or cold.

Poires pochées à la kriek
(Pears in cherry beer)

SERVES 4
4 pears
2 bottles (25 cl each) kriek / cherry beer
200 g / 7 oz caster sugar
2 cinnamon sticks (or a good pinch of ground cinnamon)
250 ml / 8 fl oz double cream
4 teaspoons icing sugar
4 scoops of cherry beer sorbet (see page 88)

Peel and core the pears and cut in half lengthways. Place in a saucepan with the beer, caster sugar and cinnamon. Simmer gently for about 20 minutes, until the pears are tender. Remove the pears from the liquid and leave to cool.

Boil the cooking liquid until it is reduced to a thick syrup, then leave to cool.

Whip the cream until it is thick, then beat in the icing sugar.

Slice the pears thinly lengthways, without cutting through the stalk end, then place on the serving plates and press gently into fan shapes. Pour the syrup over the pears and serve with the whipped cream and a scoop of sorbet.

Beignets aux pommes
(Apple fritters)

SERVES 4
150 g / 5 oz plain flour
200 ml / 7 fl oz milk
5 g / ¼ oz dried yeast
125 g / 4 oz sugar
4 apples
50 g / 2 oz butter
pinch of ground cinnamon
vegetable oil for frying
icing sugar, for dusting

Sift 100 g / 3½ oz of the flour into a bowl, gradually blend in the milk, add the yeast and 25 g / 1 oz of the sugar and set aside.

Peel, core and dice two of the apples. Put the diced apples in a small saucepan with the remaining sugar, butter and cinnamon. Add 3 tablespoons water, cover the pan and cook over a low heat for 30 minutes. Leave to cool.

Heat the oil in a deep-fat fryer or frying pan.

Peel and core the remaining two apples and cut them into 1 cm / ½ inch slices. Toss the slices in the remaining flour, then dip them into the yeast batter. Using a fork, take the slices out of the batter and carefully drop them into the hot oil. When the batter is golden brown, lift the fritters on to a paper towel to absorb excess oil. Keep warm while you fry the remaining fritters.

To serve, divide the apple purée and fritters between four warmed plates, dust with icing sugar and serve with cream or vanilla custard.

Crème caramel with
Mandarine Napoléon
(Crème caramel with
orange liqueur)

SERVES 4
200 g / 7 oz granulated sugar
300 ml / ½ pint milk
3 oranges
2 tablespoons Mandarine Napoléon liqueur
4 eggs
75 g / 3 oz caster sugar
sprigs of mint

Put the granulated sugar in a saucepan with 75 ml / 3 fl oz water. Bring to the boil, stirring occasionally until the sugar dissolves, then boil without stirring until the mixture forms a caramel. Pour the caramel into four ramekins and leave to cool and set.

Preheat the oven to 160° C / 320° F / Gas Mark 3. Grate the zest and squeeze the juice of one of the oranges.

Put the milk in a saucepan with the orange zest and juice and the Mandarine Napoléon liqueur; bring to the boil. Whisk the eggs and sugar together in a bowl, then gradually pour the milk on to the egg mixture, whisking slowly. Pour the mixture into the ramekins over the caramel.

Put the ramekins in a deep baking dish and pour in hot water to come half way to the top of the ramekins. Put the dish in the oven and cook for about 45 minutes, or until the mixture is firm.

Leave the ramekins to cool, then chill in the refrigerator for at least 2 hours. Peel the remaining oranges and cut out the segments.

To serve, invert the crème caramel out of each ramekin on to a plate. Arrange two or three orange segments and a sprig of mint on each plate.

Terrine aux trois chocolats
(Triple chocolate terrine)

SERVES 8

75 g / 3 oz each of dark, white and milk chocolate

3 eggs, separated

3 gelatine leaves

3 tablespoons Mandarine Napoléon liqueur

300 ml / ½ pint whipping cream

    Line a 1.2 litre / 2 pint terrine mould or loaf tin with clingfilm. Melt the dark chocolate in a small bowl placed over a saucepan of hot water. Stir until smooth, then beat in one of the egg yolks.

    Soak one gelatine leaf in cold water until soft. Squeeze out the water and dissolve the gelatine in 1 tablespoon of the heated liqueur.

    Whip the egg whites until stiff. Whip one-third of the cream until it is thick but not stiff, then fold in the gelatine and liqueur. Gradually fold one-third of the whipped egg whites and the chocolate mixture into the cream mixture. Pour the mixture into the lined terrine mould and leave until set. Repeat the process with the white and milk chocolate. Leave to set for at least 4 hours, then serve in slices.

Bavarois au chocolat blanc
(White chocolate bavarois)

SERVES 4

2 gelatine leaves

225 g / 8 oz white chocolate

3 egg yolks

50 g / 2 oz caster sugar

200 ml / 7 fl oz milk

1 vanilla pod

200 ml / 7 fl oz whipping cream

Soak the gelatine leaves in cold water until they are soft. Melt 200g / 7oz of the chocolate in a small bowl placed over a saucepan of hot water.

    Beat the egg yolks with the caster sugar in a mixing bowl. Put the milk and vanilla pod in a saucepan and bring to the boil. Remove the vanilla pod. Add the gelatine and whisk into the milk. Pour the hot milk on to the egg yolk and sugar mixture and whisk until smooth. Leave the mixture to cool, then stir in the melted chocolate. Whip the cream until it is thick but not stiff, then fold gently into the chocolate mixture. Divide between four ramekins, then leave to set in the refrigerator for at least 3 hours.

    To serve, invert each ramekin onto a plate. Grate the remaining white chocolate over the top. Serve with vanilla custard and either mixed berries or orange segments.

KERANG!

GENEVER

EVERY NORTHERN EUROPEAN COUNTRY has devised a knock-out concoction of some sort to accompany their beer. The Scots and the Irish have their whisk(e)ys, the Scandinavians their akvavits, the Germans sip on their korn, the Poles and Russians on their vodkas, and Dutch and the Belgians have their genevers or Belgian gin. This is the typical Belgian aperitif and it goes superbly with fish dishes, shellfish and crustacea but, best of all, beer.

Since Belgo stocks a huge selection of Belgian beers, we could not resist the temptation to make our bartenders' lives even more complicated by doing the same with our genever list. Belgo has some 30-odd genevers, most available for the first time in the UK. We decided not to carry the usual spirits that other restaurants do, not through arrogance, but simply to remain purer to the beerhall concept: beer and schnapps, that's it. OK OK, and a little wine. (In Belgium it is not uncommon for some beer bars to flatly refuse to serve anything else. We dare you to ask for a Coke or a mineral water! Once, when we did, we were told, *"Enze Bier ... Enze Aquarium"*!)

Genever (also called jenever or peket) can be traced back to the early 17th century in what is now French Flanders. The oldest recipe though has been traced back to 1552 when a certain Dutch chap called Philippus Hermanni wrote in his book *A Concise Book on Distilling*: "the Aqua Juniperus is the product of distilling wine using crushed juniper berries." This method came as a result of the harsh weather conditions in the Low Countries, which made wine production virtually impossible. During the 16th century beer took over and the production of *Eaux* or spirits, using not only wine but also beer, fruit wine and cereal, became very fashionable. Several health warnings were issued about the abuse of these spirits, in particular the grain or cereal type. Some things just don't change! One needs only to look at some of the party scenes in Bruegel's paintings to understand that concern.

Today, as for most of the last 300 years, genever is a product of grain distillation (rye, wheat, maize and barley), that is predominantly flavoured with juniper berries during its dilution stage. Other main ingredients include dried curaçao orange skins, root ginger, cumin, cinnamon, aniseed, licorice and cloves.

One of the most popular brands of genever is distilled by the Braeckman family, who in 1918 established the Braeckman Distillery in the Zwalm valley of the Flemish Ardennes. The mineral sources and pure water streams of the region provided an ideal setting for water mills and the Braeckman family distillery, which is renowned for its smooth genever. The Braeckmans produce a wide range of *oude graanjenever* (old genever), a grain distillate with large amounts of malt spirit, which is stored in oak casks for several years. This type carries a distinctive grain taste, is deeper in colour and softer on the palate. *Oude Jenever Kikendief* (Chicken Thief Old Genever), usually sold in stoneware bottles, has a purer grain taste and should be served chilled, like vodka. The *jonge genever* (Young Genever) is flavoured with herbs such as juniper berries and coriander. It should be served chilled as this enhances its unique aroma.

Besides Braeckmans, Belgo also features Stoopke, Jonge Belfort and a wide range of fruit genevers made by the oddly-named Cockney's distillery. Fruit genevers only recently became popular — although the method of flavouring with fruit is ancient — simply because of their sweetness, easier-to-please taste, and a far more moderate alcohol content: usually 18% to 25% instead of the usual 40% alcohol by volume. Flavours vary from the sweeter and more exotic walnut, lychee or mandarin, to a more subtle apple or lemon.

Other speciality brands, such as Hertekamp and Peterman, are distilled by Bruggeman. The Wortegemsen Distillery, established by Albert Kint, produces a wonderful lemon pulp genever that accompanies shellfish and fish dishes quite superbly.

Belgo sells over 100 bottles of genever a week. This is why our unique, custom-made schnapps shot sticks, which can carry up to 32 chilled shots at a time, come in very handy. We also use genever in some of our traditional dishes such as *poussin à la brabançonne* and in desserts like *sorbet au geneve braeckmans au citron*. It is also very useful for marinades, especially for game and wild fowl.

Allez!

A Brief
History of Belgium

OUR BOOK WOULD NOT be complete without a flash tribute to the rich historical background of the territory known to us today as: Belgium. This beloved food and beer paradise has had as many foreign rulers as Italy has had Presidents in the last few years (Scusa!). So the idea of foreigners using Belgian soil to settle their disputes (does Waterloo ring a bell?), setting up a trade centre (European or World H.Q.'s galore), or simply the passage to Gaule and Teutonic Forests (Euro Highway Number 9 or is it 69 to Hamburg?), is nothing new to the locals who have always been too busy, getting their own state together, to notice.

P.S. DON'T MENTION WATERLOO

Mr Belgo's
HISTORICAL LOOK AT BELGIUM

HAIL CAESAR!

The first fifteen minutes of fame for Belgium came when Julius Caesar wrote: "Of all the enemies I have encountered, of all the Gauls, the Belgians were the bravest." As it happened, the Romans stuck around in Belgae for another 500 years of pure misery.

LATINS AND SAXONS

After the Romans left, the local "Belgian" Celts were forced to share the land with the rather unpleasant Teutonic tribes. From the very beginning, Belgium was to deal with this "two nations" problem: Celts and Teutons or Latins and Saxons — Flemings and Walloons.

CHARLEMAGNE WAS A BELGIAN

Europe's first great emperor, Charlemagne, was not German, not French but Belgian (he was born on Belgian soil, probably in 742). He was responsible for dividing Europe into three tribal nations. He was also semi-successful at keeping them from each other's throats. Under Charlemagne's guidance, the Belgians learned rapidly how to live between such powerful neighbours as the French and the Germans. Indeed, learning to benefit from both cultures and their riches, the Belgians quickly established themselves as serious traders.

THE FIRST BELGIAN TRADE BOOM

Between the 12th century and 16th century, the Low Countries were one of the richest places in the world. Early trade centres in Flanders, such as Bruges and Antwerp, were extremely powerful and commanded most of the European medieval trade market, particularly for wool and the rest of the textile industry.

HERE COME THE FRENCH

In the 15th century, with the arrival of the French Burgundian Court in about 1430, Belgium flourished as an an important centre for the arts and architecture under the rule of Philip the Good, and later his son, Charles the Bold. Great artists such as Jan van Eyck and Rogier van der Weyden benefited from the Court's patronage.

HERE COME THE AUSTRIANS

When Charles the Bold died in 1477, his daughter Mary married the Austrian Prince Maximilian I. Much to the annoyance of the French king, Mary died unexpectedly, thereafter leaving all the riches of the Low Countries to her Austrian husband. This marked the beginning of Austrian Hapsburg rule, a bit of war and a great deal of unrest.

In the beginning…

BELGO'S TOP
THINGS TO DO 10
WHILE IN BELGIUM

1. **VISIT THE GENTSE FEESTEN** *(the beer festival in Ghent).*
2. **SHOP AT THE MAROLLEN FLEA MARKET** *in Brussels.*
3. **BAR CRAWL IN ANTWERP.**
4. **EAT AT PIERRE WYNANT'S RESTAURANT,** *Comme chez soi.*
5. **VISIT THE ATOMIUM** *before they pull it down.*
6. **STUMBLE INTO THE** *Maison des Brasseurs (Brewers' House) on Grande Place.*
7. **TRY THE STEAK DE CHEVAL** *at the Brabançon restaurant in Brussels.*
8. **STAY IN THE ARDENNES** *for a few days.*
9. **JOG ON ÖOSTENDE BEACH** *while listening to Marvin Gay on the Walkman.*
10. **VISIT THE CENTRE BELGE DE LA BANDE DESSIGNÉE** *Comic strip museum in Brussels..*

HERE COME THE SPANIARDS

Maximilian the Austrian was succeeded by his son Philip the Handsome.(This is not a joke.) He married a Spanish princess who gave birth to Charles V in 1500. Out went the Austrians, in came the Spanish. Charles V inherited the Kingdom of Spain *and* the Holy Roman Empire. He named Brussels as the capital of the Spanish Netherlands, and during his reign, Antwerp took over from Venice as the most important trading city in all of Europe. Worn out with managing his vast territories, he retired to a monastery in 1557 leaving Austria to his brother and Spain and the Netherlands to his son.

HERE COMES THE INQUISITION

Philip II of Spain, the son of Charles V, brought in the Inquisition – which did not go down too well with the Calvinists. Most of the period from the mid-16th century to the mid-18th century was riddled with wars and social unrest. Belgium, which became part of the Austrian empire again in the early 18th century, was continuously having to deal with other people's problems: the Spanish against the French, the French against Austrians, and so on.

BELGIUM IN DEUTSCH: NON MERCI!

One of the most important events in Belgium's history took place in 1789 in Brabant province, when the Brabant people revolted against the Austrian Emperor Joseph II's plans to turn Belgium into a German-speaking State. The revolt was a complete success due to the people's united front against foreign domination. Ruling was one thing, but converting was another. This "unity" incited the people to proclaim their territory as the land of a "united Belgium". The revolt of 1789 managed to get rid of the Austrians for a short while. The

Austrians came back only to get their marching orders by Napoleon's army. Brussels and the rest of Belgium was thereafter declared French territory.

INDEPENDENCE: PART 1

The outcome of the Battle of Waterloo (1815) was significant in bringing Belgium one step closer to self determination. For better or for worse, the main foreign powers, led by Britain and Austria, joined the State of Belgium to the Republic of Netherlands and called it the United Netherlands. Later, when William I of Orange was officially appointed king, it became known as the United Kingdom of the Netherlands.

CATHOLICS AND CALVINISTS: ALL FOR ONE?

From the start this marriage had no chance: a Catholic nation was asked to live under a Protestant rule. The combination of Catholics and Calvinists never made a great cocktail. William I also made a serious mistake in declaring Dutch the official language of both States. Brussels being, and having been for a long time now, mainly French-speaking was not going to accept this. (Brussels was the capital of the Belgian State and had great influence on the rest of the country.) Revolution was imminent.

REVOLUTION AT THE OPERA

On 25 August 1830, many of Brussels' most influential citizens and radicals were attending an Opera by Auber called *Masianello* or *La Muette de Portici*, which carried a very strong nationalistic aria devoted to the love of the Fatherland. The words "far better to die than to live a wretched life in slavery and shame … away with the foreigners who laugh at

BELGO'S TOP 10 FAMOUS BELGIANS

1. **ANDRÉ PLISNIER SNR.**
   (Spitfire ace)
2. **JAN BUCQUOY** *(Film director: The Sexual life of the Belgians)*
3. **JACQUES BREL**
   (Singer and poet)
4. **ADOLPHE SAX**
   (Inventor of the saxophone)
5. **ENZO SCHIFFO**
   (Footballer)
6. **BENOIT POELVOORDE**
   (Actor: Man Bites Dog)
7. **HERGÉ**
   (Tintin's creator)
8. **MANNEKEN-PIS**
   (Statuette in Brussels)
9. **JOHNNY HALLIDAY**
   (Singer)
10. **DRIES VAN NOTEN**
    (Designer)

our torment!" threw the audience into a frenzy. That was it. The place went nuts and the people of Belgium had a revolution. So much for the Beatles and the Sex Pistols, eh?

INDEPENDENCE: PART 2

Exactly one month later, on 25 September, William I's Dutch troops were defeated and the people of Belgium declared themselves independent. This was made official on 4 October 1830. France, Britain, and Austria confirmed it at the London Conference on 20 July 1831 and the following day Leopold I of Saxe-Coburg, an Austrian, was proclaimed the first King of the Belgians and the independent State of Belgium. Leopold was an uncle of Queen Victoria. He had married a French woman called Louise, which pleased the French very much.

21 JULY: BELGIAN INDEPENDENCE DAY

The Belgians celebrate their independence day every year on 21 July. Belgo created Belgian National Week, making this day part of a seven-day celebration of food, drink and Belgian culture.

LEOPOLD II

Famous for his great white beard and his affair with a dancer named Chloe, the promiscuous Leopold II inherited the language disputes and in-fighting between the Flemings and the Walloons that plagued his father's reign. He did manage to take a bold step towards colonization by acquiring a piece of African land fertile with coffee, sugar, cocoa and other luxury commodities. He named it the Belgian Congo.

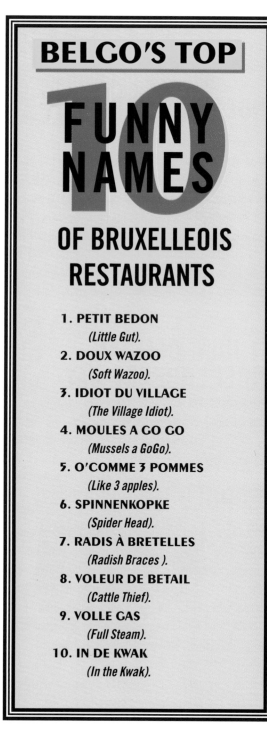

BELGO'S TOP 10 FUNNY NAMES OF BRUXELLEOIS RESTAURANTS

1. **PETIT BEDON**
   (Little Gut).
2. **DOUX WAZOO**
   (Soft Wazoo).
3. **IDIOT DU VILLAGE**
   (The Village Idiot).
4. **MOULES A GO GO**
   (Mussels a GoGo).
5. **O'COMME 3 POMMES**
   (Like 3 apples).
6. **SPINNENKOPKE**
   (Spider Head).
7. **RADIS À BRETELLES**
   (Radish Braces).
8. **VOLEUR DE BETAIL**
   (Cattle Thief).
9. **VOLLE GAS**
   (Full Steam).
10. **IN DE KWAK**
    (In the Kwak).

BELGIUM AND THE WORLD WARS

Belgium got more territory from the Germans at the end of the First World War. Leopold II's grandson, Leopold III had barely been proclaimed King before finding himself at war again when Belgium was invaded by Hitler's Germany. Belgium was declared "neutral", which provoked many to suspect Leopold III of collaboration with the Nazis. He never truly recovered from this accusation and later abdicated, giving his throne to his son Baudouin, aged 20.

BAUDOUIN

King Baudouin married a Spanish woman called Fabiola in 1960. His reign was marked with some controversy: the bloody withdrawal from the Congo (now Zaire) and his anti-abortion stance. These issues distanced him from his liberal-minded people. Baudouin was Belgium's longest reigning monarch and was succeeded by his brother Albert II.

FAST FACTS ABOUT BELGIUM

1. There are ten provinces.
2. Belgium has three official languages: Flemish, French and German.
3. The population of Belgium is 10 million (6.1 Flemish, 3.2 French, 0.7 German).
4. Brussels is the capital of the European Union and home to NATO World Headquarters.
5. Brussels has over 20,000 foreign diplomats.
6. The monetary unit is the Belgian Franc.
7. Belgium hosted the 1958 World Fair.
8. The Atomium building was designed in 1958 by André Waterkeyn and is a complete replica of the iron molecule magnified 165 billion times.

Denis and André's
TOUR OF BRUSSELS

We couldn't leave the subject of Belgium without giving you a short guided tour of our favourite restaurants, shops, people and sites. Rain or rain, we love Brussels! Allez...

Here we are smack in the middle of the Grande-Place, one of Europe's most amazing town squares. André and Denis can never decide on which way to look first.

149

(Above) Potferdoome la friture est fermée.
(Below left) Nothing like a pause-café at the
art deco Palace Falstaff.
(Right) Notre "grand-pei" Albert-Jean Niels,
owner of Le Canterbury.

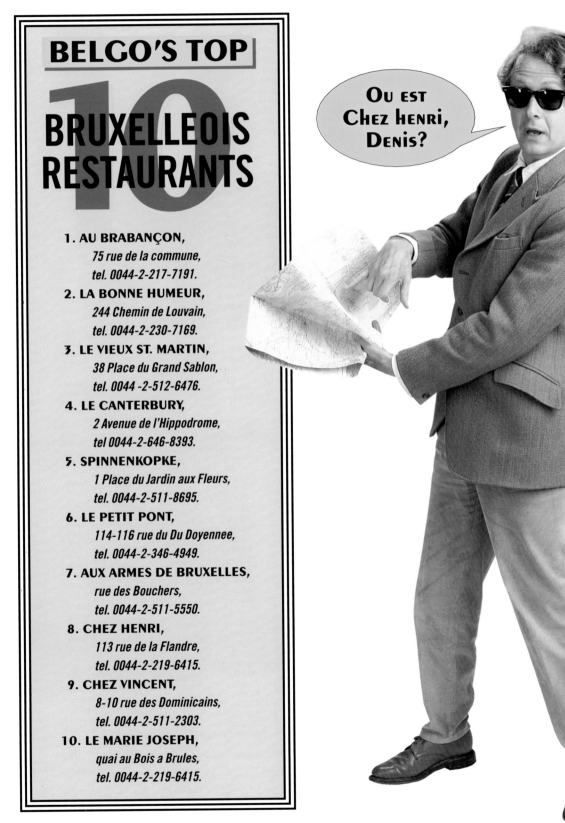

BELGO'S TOP 10 BRUXELLEOIS RESTAURANTS

1. **AU BRABANÇON,**
   75 rue de la commune,
   tel. 0044-2-217-7191.
2. **LA BONNE HUMEUR,**
   244 Chemin de Louvain,
   tel. 0044-2-230-7169.
3. **LE VIEUX ST. MARTIN,**
   38 Place du Grand Sablon,
   tel. 0044 -2-512-6476.
4. **LE CANTERBURY,**
   2 Avenue de l'Hippodrome,
   tel 0044-2-646-8393.
5. **SPINNENKOPKE,**
   1 Place du Jardin aux Fleurs,
   tel. 0044-2-511-8695.
6. **LE PETIT PONT,**
   114-116 rue du Du Doyennee,
   tel. 0044-2-346-4949.
7. **AUX ARMES DE BRUXELLES,**
   rue des Bouchers,
   tel. 0044-2-511-5550.
8. **CHEZ HENRI,**
   113 rue de la Flandre,
   tel. 0044-2-219-6415.
9. **CHEZ VINCENT,**
   8-10 rue des Dominicains,
   tel. 0044-2-511-2303.
10. **LE MARIE JOSEPH,**
    quai au Bois a Brules,
    tel. 0044-2-219-6415.

In the background is the Maison des Brasseurs on the Grande-Place. Check out the brewing museum.

(Left) After some heavy-duty shopping, stop for a beer at Le Coq. Beware – it's not for the average tourist. (Above) Then have a lobster at the Rugbyman on Place Ste. Catherine.

The Manneken-Pis off the Grande-Place
is bound to get you going.

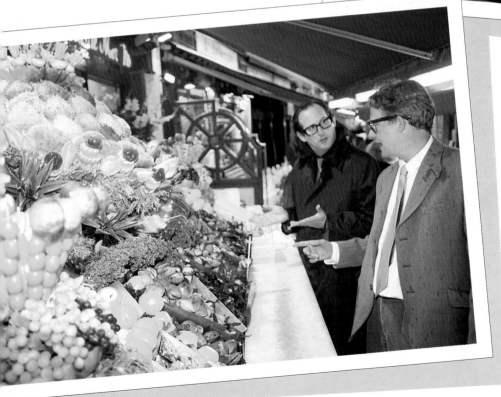

(Above) A trip to the
Maison Dandoy will
not help your diet. For
over 100 years, they
have been making
the best gingerbread
men and speculoos
and pain à la
grecque. (Left)
Denis and André
always enjoy a good
healthy selfish
shellfish debate on
the rue des
Bouchers.

(Above) A trip to Wittamer on the Place du Grand Sablon is a must for all chocoholics. (Right) Notre "grand-mei" Marie-Jeanne Lucas from the Brabançon restaurant. (Below) Toone is the oldest string-puppet theatre in the world.

CHOCOLAT

IT IS NOT UNCOMMON for André and Denis, when at one of their favourite tables in Brussels, to pass on having dessert. This is obviously not for dietary reasons but rather for a quick scive off to Wittamer on the Place du Grand Sablon, Brussel's fashionable antique quarter, for the world's best handmade chocolate praline pastries. Established by Henri Wittamer back in 1910, Wittamer is a must for any serious gastro-tourist. Every tarte, truffle, praline and cake is handcrafted in the original restaurant premises by the Wittamer family artisans, who have steered away from the temptation of global mass-production and a larger slice of the financial torte that some of their rivals have benefited from over the last decade.

One can sit on the beautiful terrace facing the Nôtre Dame du Sablon church and have delightful Belgian-style cappuccino with fresh cream and sprinkled with delicious shavings of dark Wittamer tablet chocolate. This is usually how we end our work-related excursions to Brussels. What a tough job we have! On our way to La Gare du Sud (Zuid if you are Flemish) to catch our Eurostar back to Waterloo, the assortment of fine chocolate pralines we will have bought from Wittamer for market research and development (yeah sure, says the Belgo accountant) will have long been consumed. And speaking of consumption, the 10 million Belgians rival the British in consuming the same amount of chocolate (7.4 kilos) per head per year. We can add that the quality may differ on the British side of the channel!

True Belgian chocolate pralines are handmade from the world's best chocolate, with a minimum of 70% cocoa solids, using fresh cream and butter with no preservative agents. Now we should clarify the meaning of the word praline, which is often misunderstood. The English recognize pralines as being any chocolate that is filled with a chocolate and nut paste. The Belgians, Germans and the Swiss accept any high-quality fine chocolate that is filled as a genuine "praline".

Belgo uses Belgian *Callebaut* "couverture" chocolate in all its chocolate desserts.

BELGIAN CHOCOLATIER

5 STEPS

THE ART OF TASTING FINE CHOCOLATE

1. LOOK
Make sure you see a soft shine.

2. BREAK
Snap the chocolate: a good clean break indicates a fine blend.

3. SMELL
The aroma of the clean break should be one of fragrant chocolate.

4. FEEL
The texture of the chocolate against the roof of your mouth should be creamy and velvety smooth. A grainy texture indicates poor refining.

5. EXPERIENCE
Taste fine chocolate at room temperature. The initial taste should be of a nutty, roasted chocolate flavour followed by a well-blended sweetness.

Stillekens OEN

BELGO'S TOP
10
SLANG
BRUXELLEOIS

1. **POTTEPEI**
   (silly man or drinking buddy)
2. **MEI OR PEI**
   (pal or mate)
3. **KIEKENFRETER**
   (chicken eater)
4. **STOEFFE NEK**
   (poser)
5. **BOLLEKE**
   (glass for De Koninck beer)
6. **OMNUZEL**
   (idiot)
7. **STOEMELINGS**
   (on the quiet)
8. **POTFERDOOME**
   (damn, blast)
9. **SMEERLAP**
   (bastard)
10. **STILLEKENS OEN**
   (nice and easy does it)

OK, so this is not the greatest scenic shot from the Atomium, but heck, you've got to see it to believe it. Built in 1958 for the World Fair.

Let's be honest, Denis and André snuck into 1st class for this shot only. Eurostar to Brussels, Brussels to Belgo, eh pei, c'est le paradis!

HOME AT LAST!

INDEX

ACKNOWLEDGEMENTS

Denis and André wish to thank the following people and Spirits for making this book possible:

A giant special thanks to all our kitchen chefs team (past and present). In particular Phillipe Blaise for compiling all our recipes. Also Richard Coates, Charles Noorland, Muir Pickens, Brian Sullivan, Carlton Dennis and the rest of the kitchen crew. Also thanks to Bobby for getting us going. Nest Mertens, Albert-Jean Niels, Marie-Jeanne Lucas, Miguel and Titje for depth and knowledge on the material. Katherina Ujlaki and Mary Norman for the support, research and great time management. John Lawrence Jones and Stephen Aland for fab food and D n' A shots. Phil Starling for Belgo shots and Simon Wheeler for the mussels on a rope photograph. Frank "ping-pong" Schott outer sleeve shot of D n' A . Uli Sigg for styling, shooting and bass. Susan Haynes, Nick Clark, Maggie Ramsay and Laura Washburn at W&N. The Senate and Nigel Soper for graphics. John Codling for all original artwork and logo. Michael Jackson for foreword and support, Debbie Woodcock and Melanie Ellis press. A huge thanks to the best management team in da world: André Blais, Tim Power, Chris Burton, Tim Warner, Myriam Mavros, Danny Bjelcevic, Zoe Adjey, Craig Truter, Luigi Clerici, Suzette Tegally, André Delanchy, and Deon van Niekerk Aber, Simon. Also big thanks to Jacky Kitching and Graeme Noble for getting Centraal through the heat. Major thanks to Richard Koch for believing in us and Sir Paul Judge for patience. Monique Van den Hurk for brilliant future designs and architecture and Quentin Reynolds for colours. Also Anand Zenz and Ron Arad for Noord and Centraal. Chris at the Ivy for inspiration. Meyer, Meike, Uwe, Robert, Dr Mathesius of Taschen Köln and Jonathan from Paul Smith.

Personal thanks from Denis to: my wife Danka and Egg, the best brother in the world Ptit' Dé, Franek and Wisia, Tomek, Jasia, Piotr, Maman et Papa, André, Flynn, Camille, Christian "Big Bucks", Nathalie, "Mighty Max", Nadia et Alexandre, Ben, Estelle and Jean et Sophie, Marc and Caroline et Sebastien, Steve and Victoria et Natasha. HP for keeping me sane and André for keeping me insane and putting up with it!

Personal thanks from André to Ezme, my wife, for being a loving critic of my cooking; my mother, Jenny, for honing my palate with tender Carbonades Flamandes; my father for teaching me to eat brown shrimps without removing the heads; my step-father Nils for eating as many moules as me; my Belgian grandmother, Gigi, for passing on the secrets of Belgian home cooking; my niece Alice for enjoying Belgo moules, aged three; my sister Maryse for her delicious Soupe Verte; my brother bobby for always staying one step ahead of the competition; my sisters Annabel and Sophie for having trawled the Brussels eateries with me; my friend and partner Denis for still being there eleven years later; and the friends who believed in Belgo; John Toosey and his Salade Liegeoise and a perfect frite; Nick Reynolds, the Brown Fairy; Richard Koch and Sir Paul Judge for putting their money where our mouths were; Mandy for teaching me office manners; Dr A. Mordecai for his spiritual council; Barry McMurdoch for teaching me to take risks; Jurgen and Katherina for "another" perspective; Raynold for looking after Charlie for two years; and last but not least all the Belgo team who continue to make it what it is now.

First published in 1997 by George Weidenfeld & Nicolson Ltd

This paperback edition first published in 1998 by Phoenix Illustrated Orion Publishing Group, Orion House, 5, Upper St. Martin's Lane London WC2H 9EA

British Library Cataloguing-in-Publication Data A catalogue record for this book is available from the British Library

ISBN 0753804905

Brilliant design by Nigel Soper

MERCI TOUT LE MONDE!

BELGO SAYS AU REVOIR AND HOPE TO SEE YOU SOON!